I0416198

Create SPACE

get what you *really* want at work

Craig S. Gilden

Cory Sherb

To order additional copies, please visit

http://frozenyams.com/CreateSPACE

The examples in this book depict fictional situations and characters inspired by real events.

Copyright © 2006 by Craig S. Gilden and Cory Sherb

ISBN 978-1-4116-8678-6

CONTENTS

Acknowledgements   **5**

Preface   **7**

Introduction   **11**

Your Interface with your Organization Determines your Success   12

You Make the Box You Work Within   13

SPACE → Sensemaking → Less Frustration → More Satisfaction   15

SPACE: A behavior-based approach   15

S – P – A – C – E   16

Introducing…AirSPACE   18

AirSPACE: Tool Shop Utilization Report Example   19

Survey   **23**

What is "Your Organization?"   24

Symptoms of High Friction Organizations   24

Organizational Mechanics   26

Working in an Organization is as Easy as Riding a Bicycle   26

Organizational Mechanics – Definitions   29

The Heart of Organizational Mechanics: The Law of Conversation of Organizational Energy   33

Friction is the Organization's Problem; Heat is Your Problem   40

Survey – Conclusions   42

AirSPACE: Tool Shop Utilization Report Example - Survey Implications   42

Probe   **45**

Friction: What it Is and What it Does   46

Two types of Friction: Ambient and Point Sources   48

Ambient Sources of Friction   48

Ambient Source #1: Bureaucratic Processes   49

Ambient Source #2: Functional Chimneys or Silos   51

Ambient Source #3: Negative attitude towards Subordinates   52

Point Sources of Friction   56

The Finer Points of Friction   59

Why Friction Persists in Organizations   61

Heat Creation is No Longer Just Painful   64

Probe - Conclusions   65

AirSPACE: Tool Shop Utilization Report Example   66
    – Probe Implications

Assess   **69**

Self-Righteousness – the Core of All Heat   70

The Goals-Righteousness Model   71

Self-Righteousness Explored   80

The Path to Controlling your Self-Righteousness   81

Assess-Accept-Act   84

SPACEable Goals   85

Assess-Accept-Act Continued   90

Time Horizons   91

Bottom Lines   93

Integrity and Being Right – The Finer Points of Self-   95
    Righteousness

Assess-Accept-Act – The Other Two Parts   96

Conclusions for Assess-Accept-Act   99

Assess – Conclusions   99

AirSPACE: Tool Shop Utilization Report Example   100
    - Assess Implications

Create SPACE   **103**

Invisibility   104

The Laws of Invisibility   109

The Laws of Invisibility – Law #1   111

The Laws of Invisibility – Law #2   118

The Laws of Invisibility – Law #3   122

The Laws of Invisibility – Law #4   126

The Laws of Invisibility – Law #5   131

The Laws of Invisibility – Law #6   132

The Laws of Invisibility – Law #7   136

The Laws of Invisibility – Law #8   137

Invisibility – Management Implications   139

Create SPACE – Conclusions   140

AirSPACE: Tool Shop Utilization Report Example   140
- Create SPACE Implications

Execute   **143**

Invisibility Law #8…a and b   144

Law #8a   144

Law #8b and the Credit Trap   147

SPACE Loops   148

SPACE Partners   155

Rate of SPACE Creation   160

SPACE Maps   163

Execute – Conclusions   164

AirSPACE: Tool Shop Utilization Report Example   165
- Execute Implications

Conclusion   **169**

ACKNOWLEDGEMENTS

Cory and Craig would like to thank the following: Lon Van Geloven, Ed Smith, Nick McGuire, Jocelyn Porquez, and Dave Herman for attending our seminar and giving early feedback, Sue and Scott Brodie for giving us exceptional feedback and examples of how SPACE applied in areas we had not expected – thanks to Scott for the book feedback, Kristin Borsenik for being a fan and keeping touch, Tom Miller for his editorial review, Nariman Tahir for the cover design, Diane Gilden for her endless love and support and for proofing the book – you are the best, Mike Gilden for checking out the seminar, Alan Gilden for always challenging us and for go-cart racing, Dan Gilden for encouragement and feedback, Brian Gilden for being you, Matt Arpin for the constant high energy motivation and encouragement – Craig loves you, John Shevlin for arranging our first seminar and providing us some ball centering, Brandon Brooks for feedback and examples, Jason and Patricia Stansbury for their long-time emotional support and continued intellectual involvement in the project, Kay and Robin van der Made for their holiday overtime without pay, Warren Shieh for the reality checks over IM, Dad for all of the dinners, and that which is Kristen M. Reinke.

Thanks, Ralph Ellison, for revealing our Invisibility and setting us free.

Last, but not least, thanks to Rebecca for her love (to Craig), support, and childcare services on many, many Saturdays.

Jason says: "Mr. Cory!"

PREFACE

I am Invisible at work, just like you are.

After years of bumps and bruises in my job, I read Ralph Ellison's classic novel <u>Invisible Man</u>. The similarities between the main character and me were striking. He tried hard to do the right thing for his organization but was constantly resisted and often punished despite his good intentions. It reminded me of how I felt when I only wanted to make my organization better. I realized that the story about this man, with his solid education and desire to make great things happen, was my story. He was Invisible and so was I. Each time he failed, I felt his pain because I had lived those same failures. Because the story felt so familiar, I suspected there were keys hidden in the pages which could help me figure out why I, like Ellison's narrator, continued to fail at work. But I was unsure how to find those keys.

Then I met Cory who, by coincidence, was also reading <u>Invisible Man</u>. I shared with him my frustration of being the subject of a literary classic written a half-century before I was born. As we talked, we resolved to understand how the narrator kept failing despite his desire to serve and improve his organization. We interpreted Ellison's novel as a story about how people use power and control within organizations to get what they want. The book is rich in its diverse cast of characters. A few had something in common: they knew how to use what power they possessed to get what they really wanted. It did not matter if they were at the top of their organization calling all the shots, or at the bottom grinding out their days as one of the system's cogs. The successful people were extremely effective in getting what they wanted with whatever power they had.

To the narrator, power was a locomotive that ran him over every time because he could not understand that he needed to get out of its way. To those characters who were 'successful,' power was a beam of energy which they could focus, channel, use to create their own refuge, or wield to inflict pain and damage. I was the narrator who was run over every time. I listened to the stories of others in my organization – people like you – who worked hard to do the right thing and make the organization better. We were run over more often than not.

Preface

It was striking how the characters in <u>Invisible Man</u>, even those who seemingly had little power, knew how to channel its flow, magnify it, and use it to get what they really wanted. They knew how to carve out a space for themselves and fill it with things that satisfied their wants and needs. In our own organization, we saw those same characters who knew how to get what they wanted, regardless of their position in the organization. How could we tap into their code?

Through countless lunchtime conversations, we developed theories of why the narrator continued failing in order to determine how we could be more successful. We then mapped out a method of behavior which would have saved Ellison's narrator an enormous amount of pain. We began to use those behaviors ourselves and saw that they helped us get out of the way of power when we needed to. We began to understand power, how some people effectively used it, and how others just didn't get it. We also noticed that those who knew how to use power successfully were not frustrated like so many others in the organization.

These new behaviors would have enabled Ellison's narrator to achieve results. We practiced these new behaviors over the following months and our organization responded differently to both of us. We began to successfully avoid pitfalls. However, something was missing. We felt we were giving up some things which were important to us in order to behave in ways that were 'acceptable' to our organization. We were not feeling the pain we previously felt, but we did not feel rewarded either. We turned to Ellison for more answers.

The successful characters in <u>Invisible Man</u> were very rational about what they wanted and they tuned their behaviors to achieve their goals. Whether they were working for a greater good or for their own benefit, they all tuned their behaviors to get what they wanted. Because we had not clarified what we wanted from our organization, we felt unsatisfied with our new behaviors even though they helped us successfully avoid the pain we previously felt. The key we had been missing was understanding what we really wanted. Cory and I dug deeper. We developed new theories and applied them to the characters in Ellison's classic and to others in our own organization. The SPACE method was now complete.

The behaviors which caused the narrator's failures are timeless, as Ellison recognized them so long ago. The ways the narrator kept failing were the same ways I kept failing. You may be failing in these same ways. Whereas <u>Invisible Man</u> presents the behaviors that lead to failure, SPACE presents the behaviors that lead to success. SPACE can make the best out of your daily experiences at work. It will show you how to make the greatest impact that your organization will accept. It is a win-win approach: your organization will get what it wants and you will get what you want.

Life is different than it was when we did not understand the nuances of working successfully in our organization. We now better understand what people want at work. We understand what we *truly* want. We no longer waste energy pursuing goals that are not important to us. The tools we developed are straightforward and useful, withstanding test after test at work and at home. We hope you will find it as useful as we have in getting what is important to you in your life.

INTRODUCTION

Are you getting what you *really* want at work?

When you are getting what you *really* want at work,

- You aren't frustrated.
- You don't regularly complain about work.
- You don't get angry about your job or about things that happen at work.

When you are getting what you *really* want at work,

- You feel like you have the freedom to do your job in the way you want.
- Amid stress and high pressure, you feel a certain calm because you are not fighting needless battles that drain your energy.
- You feel like you are making an impact in your organization in the best way you can.

When you are getting what you *really* want at work,

- You can focus your energy outside of work on the people and the things that you love.
- You can better concentrate on your passions because you take more energy home with you instead of spending it all at work.

It's time for you to start getting what you *really* want at work.

When you read a self-improvement book or go to a motivational seminar, you feel charged and energized. You are ready to unleash the greatness within yourself and spread it throughout your organization. You are ready to develop new habits that make you more effective and more satisfied. Unfortunately, nobody else in your organization has experienced the same change you have. You are energized, but your colleagues still have the motivation and enthusiasm they had before you read your book or attended your seminar. Over time, despite your best intentions and efforts, you return to your original state of equilibrium.

SPACE is more *illuminating* than it is *motivating*: it provides a solid foundation of learning and understanding rather than a fleeting boost in motivation. SPACE is unique because it does not expect anyone around you to change; it *expects* everyone to remain the same. It does not require others to want the same positive changes or personal improvements that you want. As a result, this approach does not set unrealistic expectations for you to successfully apply what you learn.

SPACE will change your perspective about how organizations operate. You will be surprised at how things that were previously frustrating will no longer seem important. You will expend less energy in all the clichés that describe wasted time and effort: spinning your wheels, beating your head against walls, and going nowhere fast. Your new perspective will increase your satisfaction at work. You will be a *better* contributor. Your organization will appreciate *how* you do your job in addition to the great job you already do. You will increase your effectiveness while reducing the effects of the negative energy we all feel at times within our organizations. Your entire work environment will improve when you know that your energy is helping you and your organization get what you both *really* want.

This book shows you how to clarify, or even determine, what is *truly* important to you. It provides ready-to-use tools and strategies to attain those things. You will see how to come home each day with the satisfaction that you are part of a win-win agreement in which your organization gets what it wants from you and you get what you want from your organization.

Your Interface with your Organization Determines your Success

Just as every individual has his or her own personality, each organization has its own personality. Each organization wants things in different ways. *How* work gets done can be almost as important (or, in some organizations, *more* important) than the actual work that gets done. Have you ever been frustrated by *how* someone did a job for you? Organizations, like individuals, want work done in a particular way, and they sometimes place enormous importance on *how* you do your job. If you try to give your organization something in a way it does not appreciate, you will experience resistance and frustration.

Because organizations can be particular about *how* they want work to be done, they value various skills and work styles differently. For example, methodical organizations value a different set of skills than high-energy organizations. If your organization values your work style, you will feel rewarded and fulfilled. However, if there is a mismatch between your natural style and the styles your organization appreciates, you will feel frustrated. The match between your style and the styles valued by your organization is an important factor in your success.

Fortunately, even if your style does not naturally suit your organization, you can still be successful. All you must do is manage your *interface* with your organization. Your interface is your every day attitudes, actions and, ultimately, your behaviors. It is how you do your work, approach problems, express differing ideas, and try to make great things happen. You are smart, well qualified, and motivated. You have great intentions. If you are not successful or fulfilled, it is probably just a problem of your interface with your organization. SPACE will show you how to manage your interface so you can work *in a way your organization appreciates*. When you do this, you will find that you will get what you *really* want from work.

> Managing your <u>interface</u> with your organization is your key to success.

SPACE does not intend for you to change your ideas or values. This book is focused on your *interface* with your organization. Managing your interface is the key to ensuring that your organization accepts your ideas and the great work you want to contribute. When you interface properly with your organization, it will reward you in many ways. You will increase your ability to make things happen and will feel more freedom and empowerment to turn your ideas into reality. When you properly manage your interface, you will experience the benefits of a bigger box.

You Make the Box You Work Within

Everyone has a box which they work within. You cannot see your box but you feel it every day. The size of your box impacts every aspect of your life at work. It determines how much responsibility you are given, how much authority you have to make things happen, and how much leeway you are granted to do your job.

When you have a large box, you can accomplish more within your organization. A larger box means you have more maneuvering room. You can focus on a wider variety of goals. You will be more satisfied with your job because you will *feel* truly empowered. Of course, the opposite is true. If you have a small box, it will be difficult to get things done. Your management will not trust you and will tend to micromanage you. You will feel frustrated at the end of the day and will be dissatisfied with your work.

The size of your box varies depending on your organization. If you are in an organization that empowers its employees, you will have a large box to work within. You may have authority to make large purchase decisions or to make various commitments to customers. If you are in an organization that closely manages its employees, you will have a small box to work within. As a result, you may frequently be required to go to your management to get approval to make decisions and take actions.

Other factors impact the size of your box in your organization. Some job functions within a company are allowed to make a wider range of decisions than others. Engineers at an engineering company may have a bigger box to work within than marketing employees. Computer programmers will have a bigger box at a software company than a person in the mailroom. Those higher within an organization's hierarchy have bigger boxes than those lower in the organization. Your supervisor can make a wider range of decisions than you and is not required to get as many approvals as you for making decisions.

All these factors influence the size of your box and are somewhat out of your immediate control. However, your actions, behaviors, and *how* you perform your job are large factors within your control that determine the size of your box. If your management trusts you because you do your work in a way that is comfortable to them, you will have a bigger box. They will not scrutinize your decisions closely and will review your work less frequently. However, if your management views you as someone whom they cannot trust to behave according to their expectations, you will feel tighter bounds around you. They will supervise you more closely, require you to get approval for more basic decisions, and will not let you interact with people outside of your organization in sensitive situations. You will have a smaller box.

The size of your box is key to your success and satisfaction within your organization. Your box reflects how your organization views you and your ability to get things done *in the way it wants you to do them*. **Your box at work defines what you are capable of doing within your organization** *from your organization's perspective*.

> To be successful and get what you *really* want, you must increase the size of your box.

You expand the size of your box by doing the great work you do in the way your organization wants you to do it. Your organization must appreciate your interface. When you ensure that your behaviors are appropriate for your organization, you will increase the size of your box, enabling you to get what you *really* want.

SPACE → Sensemaking → Less Frustration → More Satisfaction

It is difficult to manage your interface when you are frustrated with how your organization operates. What your organization *says* is not always what it *really* wants. You may feel like you are given impossible tasks to complete with inadequate resources. You may see promotion decisions that baffle you. These mixed messages cause confusion and irritation for you and your colleagues. When you are frustrated, you are more apt to act in ways your organization does not appreciate.

To effectively manage your interface, you must understand what your organization *really* wants. SPACE's behavior-based approach helps you understand the motives of your organization and of the individuals within it. SPACE provides a framework for considering different possibilities regarding what people *really* want despite what they *say* they want. These alternate possibilities explain why confusing situations happen as they do. Previously puzzling events in your organization will make sense in ways they never did before.

SPACE: A Behavior-Based Approach

The five-step SPACE approach focuses intensely on behaviors – both your behaviors and others'. Behaviors provide reliable evidence which you can use to evaluate what someone *really* wants. Organizations, through Mission Statements or guidelines of preferred behaviors, *say* they want certain things, but then do not consistently act in ways to make you believe that they *really* want what they say they want. Behaviors show you whether words are aligned with actions. It is easy for someone to *say* they want something. It is different for someone to act according to what they say they want.

For example, an organization may say they want their employees to be customer-focused. If that organization rewards employees for providing exceptional customer service, there is confirmation through behaviors that it, in fact, values customer service. If, however, someone provides exceptional customer service and is *not* rewarded, exceptional customer service may not be what the organization *really* wants. Further, if someone uses company resources to make a customer happy and is punished for 'misusing' resources, the organization may not truly value exceptional customer service. Behaviors, over time, are reliable indicators about what individuals and organizations *really* want, regardless of the words they say.

SPACE also focuses on *your* behaviors. If you are not experiencing the success of which you are capable, your organization is resisting something about your interface. An organization will reward you only if you behave in ways that it accepts. If you wish to increase the size of your box and get what you *really* want, your behaviors must be consistent with behaviors which are acceptable to your organization.

If you feel resistance when you try to make positive change, it may have nothing at all to do with your *ideas*. Organizations value the work that gets done *as well as how work gets done*. Your interface must be acceptable to your organization in order for you to make things happen, get rewarded, and get what you *really* want.

S – P – A – C – E

The five steps in SPACE are:

S – Survey	Survey your organization
P – Probe	Probe for Sources of Organizational Friction
A – Assess	Assess your own goals
C – Create Space	Create Space to do what's important to you
E – Execute	Execute your plan Invisibly

SPACE begins by **S**urveying your organization to understand how easily work can be accomplished. SPACE compares your organization with a mechanical object: a bicycle. Just as a bicycle has friction, organizations also have Friction. When you understand the Friction in your organization, you can adjust your expectations of what can be accomplished and plan a more effective approach to your job. The amount of Friction in your organization tells you a great deal about what your organization *really* wants and the behaviors it values. Understanding how much Friction is present is key to understanding the interface you must have with your organization.

Survey considers how energy flows within an organization. Each organization is powered by its employees, and every employee has the potential to contribute their energy to make great products and services. Survey shows how Friction can cause that energy to be wasted.

Introduction

Understanding how energy moves within an organization allows you to understand how your behaviors contribute to better products and services or to the waste of energy. Understanding the energy flow enables you to create win-win outcomes, maximizing your impact and that of those around you.

Survey is a valuable sense-making tool which will lower the frustration you feel at work. When things happen in your organization that do not make sense, it is not because the organization is behaving irrationally. More likely, there are understandable reasons for these confusing occurrences. You may not have the information you need to make sense of what you see. Survey fills in the missing information about events in your organization, lowering your frustration about situations that currently confuse and irritate you.

The second step in SPACE is to **P**robe your organization to understand what Sources of Friction exist. You must carefully choose and execute the proper interface when working around Friction. Friction exists in organizations for specific reasons and can be dangerous to those who work hard to make positive change.

Sources of Friction reveal your organization's unspoken goals, which are different from its stated goals and mission. To increase the size of your box and get what you *really* want from your organization, you must give it what it *really* wants. Probe shows you how to determine what is truly important to your organization.

The third step in SPACE is to **A**ssess your own goals within your organization. There are many things you may want from your organization: a raise, a promotion, job security, or a technical challenge. Some of these are more important than others. You must clearly understand what you *really* want so you can keep focused in the midst of the challenges your organization provides. When you understand your true goals, it is easy to manage your interface to maximize the impact of your energy.

Assess presents Self-Righteousness, the most destructive stumbling block that wastes energy and causes needless frustration for everyone within an organization. It causes you to act out of emotion without regard to the consequences of your actions. Self-Righteousness causes you to abandon things you do not realize are important to you and fight for something you do not really want. When that happens, everyone loses: your energy is wasted and your organization will not reward you for behaving in this manner.

The fourth step in SPACE is to **C**reate Space to do what is important to you. Create Space shows you how to manage your interface with your organization. Through the first three steps in SPACE, you will learn what your organization *really* wants and what you *really* want. Create Space shows you how to deliver and achieve those things in a way that is acceptable to your organization.

Create Space introduces the concept of Invisibility. Acting Invisibly is an effective way of working which maximizes the usefulness of your energy. Everyone in an organization is Invisible to someone. Invisibility sets up dynamics which you must carefully manage through your interface. The best way to deliver what your organization *really* wants is to act Invisibly. To navigate your organization's Friction, SPACE provides the Laws of Invisibility: a complete toolkit for effectively managing your interface.

The fifth and final step in SPACE is to **E**xecute your plan to get what you *really* want in a way that continually gives your organization what it *really* wants. SPACE is a continuous process. You must remember to practice it when you experience frustration *and* success within your organization. The tools provided in Execute keep SPACE in the forefront of your mind as you increase your ability to get things done. Execute will help you remember to act Invisibly while you continuously increase the size of your box.

Introducing... AirSPACE

A company called AirSPACE is a useful setting for illustrating the SPACE concepts. Situations frequently arise at AirSPACE that clearly demonstrate how SPACE principles apply to life within organizations.

AirSPACE is a large manufacturer of small jets. AirSPACE employs thousands of people at its main manufacturing facility and engineering offices. It is an old company with a rich history and a reputation over the years for producing great products. However, AirSPACE has a deeply engrained corporate culture that is not always accepting of change. In recent years, AirSPACE has seen increased competition and, as a result, its profits have steadily declined. While it is still financially healthy, AirSPACE's long-term prospects do not look as bright as they once did.

AirSPACE is a High-Friction Organization. The company, through its mission statement and corporate communications, tells its employees that it wants and values certain behaviors, like out-of-the-box thinking. Unfortunately, it does not reward these behaviors; instead, it resists or punishes employees who exhibit them. There are many competing agendas within AirSPACE. Sometimes it seems as if the organization *wants* its major departments to fight to protect their individual territories. The product development department seems to constantly bicker with the marketing team and the manufacturing group. People seem amiable in meetings but frequently leave them with no intention of meeting commitments made to other groups.

AirSPACE is an extreme case of a High-Friction Organization, but you will recognize things that happen there. Your own organization may exhibit some of the very same behaviors. Throughout this book, AirSPACE will provide the setting for situations which will clearly demonstrate how to apply SPACE principles.

Example: **AirSPACE**
Tool Shop Utilization Report

Andrew
Supervisor

|

Bryant
Engineer

Each chapter will conclude with a situation involving AirSPACE's new Tool Shop. This example will be used to apply SPACE concepts and determine the implications that each phase has on the situation.

Bryant is an engineer for AirSPACE. He is intelligent, takes pride in his company, and delivers high-quality work. Bryant is a 'do-the-right-thing' person who really wants AirSPACE to be successful and profitable. He gets frustrated with the politics of this big company and dislikes wasting time and effort. As such, Bryant has not always been as patient with AirSPACE as its corporate culture requires. His ideas and his desire to produce thorough and high-quality work are not always rewarded and appreciated.

Bryant has a wife and three teenaged children. His family is his highest priority in his life. He works hard for AirSPACE but makes sure he arrives home to his family in time to give his energy and attention to being a great husband and father.

Bryant has been practicing SPACE for a year and is effectively applying the new concepts. He reacts to things differently than he did in the past; he has modified his interface. He sees positive results from his new methods of operating: he gets more work done in a way that AirSPACE appreciates, his box is bigger, and he feels little frustration and pressure.

Introduction

Bryant works in a building that houses AirSPACE's new Tool Shop. Last year, AirSPACE spent $25 million to build a state-of-the-art facility for creating specialized aircraft parts. They staffed the Tool Shop with 35 skilled machinists to run the new equipment. Because of this investment, AirSPACE's upper management asked the Tool Shop to report on the state of the facility. Bryant's supervisor, Andrew, asked him to develop a one-page report showing how effectively the new Tool Shop is being used.

Bryant has worked in the Tool Shop since it was built, so he knows what is important for determining its efficiency. He used a methodical approach to develop graphs and charts that quickly and clearly showed how the facility was operating. He shared it with his colleagues and they were impressed by how effectively it demonstrated the Tool Shop's performance. If his management really wanted to use this report to manage the Tool Shop and improve its performance over time, it was effective for doing just that. Unfortunately, Bryant's report did not tell a positive story. By many measures, the Tool Shop was not maximizing AirSPACE's return on its investment. Costs and scrap rates were higher than necessary and efficiencies were lower than they could have been. While Bryant's report was a great tool that would help his management drive improvements to the facility, there would be resistance to using it because it told a less-than-pretty story.

Andrew is one year away from retirement. His position gives him good pay, good benefits, and little stress. He has experienced years of pain within AirSPACE's High-Friction environment and his motivation and drive have been worn down. He has found a comfort level in his current job and chooses to follow the path of least resistance. A few conversations with Andrew will tell you that he is tired and looking forward to his retirement.

In a meeting of his small department, Bryant presented his one-page report to Andrew. Andrew looked at Bryant's report and sat quietly in front of the group. He shook his head and said: "You know, this isn't really what I had in mind. I wanted something that shows better numbers than this. Let me give you an example, Bryant. I know that the Engine Manufacturing Facility has the capacity to make 10,000 engines per year. Now, they only make 1,000 engines per year, but they advertise their full capacity on their main management reports. Their capacity has nothing to do with their performance, but senior management sees the big number, they love Engine's facility and they allow Engine to operate as they please. That's what I want. I want you to come up with measures that look good. If you have to count the number of blades of grass in front of our office, that's what I want you to do – just make it look good."

Introduction

If you are surprised by Andrew's boldness in being so forward about requesting a report that simply 'looks good,' know that these experiences are representative of life in a High-Friction Organization.

Bryant is now faced with a decision. He has worked for three full days to develop his report. He knows it is the right tool for what AirSPACE management said they wanted. He knows that what Andrew is asking for will not efficiently drive the Tool Shop towards increased profitability. How should he respond to Andrew?

Bryant could choose many different approaches. He could fly off the handle and berate Andrew in front of the department for his lack of ethics and integrity. He could respectfully refuse to change the report. He could reluctantly agree to do just as Andrew requested.

At the end of each phase of SPACE, the new concepts will be applied to the Tool Shop Utilization Report example. You will see the implications that SPACE has for Bryant's decision of how he should address Andrew's request.

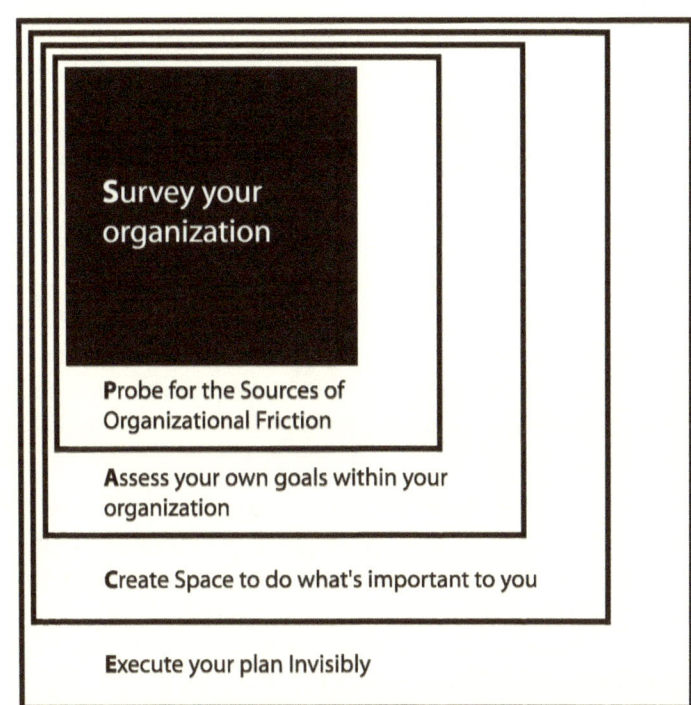

S

Survey your organization

Probe for the Sources of Organizational Friction

Assess your own goals within your organization

Create Space to do what's important to you

Execute your plan Invisibly

Work is accomplished differently within different organizations. Some of the energy you expend to make great things happen will do just that: make positive changes that result in better products and services or increased profitability. Unfortunately, some of your energy will be wasted. The structure of your organization determines if your energy will be used efficiently. Your organization's structure tells you *how* work can be accomplished and, ultimately, how your organization *wants* work accomplished. You must understand *how* your organization wants you to do your work.

Survey will show you how work is accomplished so you can choose the appropriate interface with your organization. The Survey chapter will:

- Define "your organization" to frame the Survey discussion.
- List symptoms to help you determine the amount of Friction in your organization.
- Explain Organizational Mechanics, the SPACE framework for understanding how work is accomplished.

When you understand how work is done in your organization, you can tune your interface to deliver your work in a way that maximizes your impact. Frustration and aggravation will waste less of your energy. You will *feel* better about working within your organization and your organization will appreciate your new interface. It will reward you by giving you a bigger box.

What is "Your Organization?"

"Your organization" can mean many things and it changes depending upon the situation. In a large company, you may be in a section, which is part of a department, which is part of a division, and so on. Generally, "your organization" means: "the group you work within most frequently." However, you may work in cross-functional teams with members from other areas of your company. In that situation, consider your organization to be a collection of those areas. When you consider "your organization," choose the definition that makes the most sense for the current circumstances.

In Survey, you will evaluate your entire organization. You must perform a separate Survey for each different work group with which you interface. Start Survey at the lowest level by surveying your immediate work group. Repeat Survey at the highest level, considering your entire company as a single entity. Finally, survey groups in between if you work with other teams. Survey requires you to consider many different levels of your organization.

Symptoms of High-Friction Organizations

SPACE concepts apply to all organizations, but are especially effective for High-Friction Organizations. Friction is dangerous because it will keep you from getting what you *really* want. Friction is the culprit that wastes your energy and well-intentioned efforts. When you know how much Friction is in your organization, you can better manage your interface. Without yet defining "Friction," look at the following list of symptoms of High-Friction Organizations:

Symptoms of High-Friction Organizations:

1) The organization does not value employees' opinions.
2) Employees cannot freely bring forth problems.
3) Employees lie or massage data.
4) There are turf battles between departments.
5) Project reviews are seen as an opportunity for employees to get punished.
6) Management makes arbitrary changes at will.
7) Employees are punished when they make a political misstep.
8) Employees are not punished for exhibiting bad behavior.
9) Workers are not held accountable for their actions and results.
10) The organization values behavior over results.
11) Employees are easily blamed for problems.
12) Seemingly simple tasks take more time than they should.
13) Purchase decisions take longer than they should.
14) The internal job transfer process is inconsistent and unclear.

How many of the fourteen symptoms do you recognize in your organization? It is not important to know exactly how much Friction is in your organization, but it *is* important to know if you are in a Low-Friction Organization or a High-Friction Organization. If you recognize 5 or fewer of the symptoms, you are in a Low-Friction Organization. If you recognize 8 or more of the symptoms, you are in a High-Friction Organization. In High-Friction Organizations, you must carefully choose your *interface* to increase the size of your box. If your interface is acceptable, you will work in a way that avoids creating Heat, which High-Friction Organizations hate. Creating Heat will shrink your box and keep you from getting what you *really* want.

"Friction" and "Heat" are terms from SPACE's framework of how organizations operate called "Organizational Mechanics." Organizational Mechanics increases your effectiveness in three ways. First, it helps you understand the effects Friction has on how work is accomplished. Second, instead of wasting energy, Organizational Mechanics shows you how to channel more of your energy into work that matters. Finally, Organizational Mechanics explains why inconsistent events occur within your organization, reducing your frustration and enabling you to work more effectively.

Organizational Mechanics

Organizational Mechanics explains how work gets done within organizations. It shows how much Useful Work *can* be accomplished. Organizational Mechanics assumes there is a finite amount of energy available to an organization for making its products and services and increasing profitability. That energy is present within each of the organization's employees. Organizational Mechanics defines the rules which govern how much energy is channeled into worthwhile pursuits and how much is lost. These rules determine and explain situations such as how promotions are given, who receives desirable assignments, and how work is accomplished.

Organizational Mechanics applies physics terms to organizations, helping you understand how they operate. Think of your organization as a jigsaw puzzle. If you are missing critical pieces to the puzzle, the picture may not make sense. This can be very frustrating if you need to understand the picture to accomplish something. Organizational Mechanics illuminates confusing situations, fitting the pieces together to make a cohesive image. When the picture makes sense, confusing decisions are no longer mysterious and you will feel less frustrated. *Feeling* less frustrated is a critical part of managing your interface to increase the size of your box.

To learn Organizational Mechanics, consider how organizations are similar to a simple mechanical object: a bicycle. By comparing an organization to a bicycle, you will see how physics terms readily apply to organizations to show how work is accomplished.

Working in an Organization is as Easy as Riding a Bicycle

If you leave your bicycle in the rain and snow for the winter, it will need maintenance before you can enjoy riding it again. The chain and wheel may be rusty from exposure. When you climb on the bicycle and pedal, you will hear the wheels squeaking because of rust. If there is a lot of rust, the squeaking will be loud and the bicycle will be difficult to pedal. It is difficult to pedal because of friction. Friction occurs when rough or non-lubricated objects contact each other during movement. Friction creates heat and wastes some of the energy you use to pedal. You will expend a lot of energy and effort to get somewhere

– more energy than if there were no friction in the bicycle. Does this sound like your organization? Do you feel like you expend more energy than you think you should to accomplish your goals?

If there is only a small amount of rust in the bicycle, friction is low and you will not lose much energy as you pedal. If there is a large amount of rust in the bicycle, you will experience a high level of friction and will need to work harder to travel the same distance than if your bicycle was free of rust. In other words, when there is more friction, *you must work harder to get to the same place and achieve the same results than if you had no friction.* When friction is present in your bicycle, some of the energy you want to use to get somewhere is simply wasted.

The same is true with your organization. If your organization has a high level of Friction, you must work harder to achieve the same results than if your organization had less Friction. Some of your energy will achieve results, but some will simply be wasted. It is frustrating to work in an organization filled with Friction. You cannot see Friction but you feel its effects. You are constantly impeded by something you cannot see. Because you cannot see it, it is difficult to understand why your energy is wasted so often.

Friction is bad for any mechanical system. You must regularly change the oil in your car because, if you do not, the oil will not lubricate your engine properly and keep the friction low. Friction and heat will increase and will eventually destroy the engine. Likewise, in the bicycle example, you can continue to ride your bicycle even if there is a lot of friction. However, that friction will damage you bicycle over time and, eventually, your bicycle will break. Friction, in the end, causes failure.

A High-Friction Organization, like a rusty bicycle, requires an excessive amount of energy. Employees will exert significant effort to accomplish the most mundane tasks. This extra energy required to overcome Friction means that the organization cannot accomplish as much work. Employees will be frustrated because, like riding a rusty bicycle, they must work unnecessarily hard to go somewhere. Employees in Lower-Friction Organizations will channel more of their energy into Useful Work. The Lower-Friction Organization will deliver better products and services and generate greater profits.

Companies that perpetuate negative behaviors resulting from Organizational Friction will find themselves increasingly uncompetitive. Eventually, through layoffs or other severe measures, a company may finally change its culture and eliminate some of its Friction. Organizations which do not change quickly enough will discover that they cannot produce their products or services at the lowest cost. Friction, in the end, causes failure.

> ## Example: *AirSPACE*
> ### *An Example of Organizational Friction*
>
> **Bryant**
> Engineer

Last year, Bryant was asked to purchase a portable projector for making presentations with a laptop computer. He thought this would be an easy assignment. However, his experience with this purchase became a key moment for highlighting the frustration and loss of energy and motivation caused by Organizational Friction.

AirSPACE's purchasing guidelines required Bryant to:

1) Write a business case to justify the purchase.
2) Review the business case with his supervisor.
3) Find someone with an approved source of funds with which he could pay for the projector.
4) Convince the person with the approved funding to use the funding for this purpose.
5) Contact the purchasing department to find the list of preferred vendors from whom AirSPACE may purchase equipment.
6) Contact three vendors to receive price quotes.
7) Take a training class to use an old and dated computer system for entering the purchase information.
8) Enter the purchase information into the endless screens of the dated computer system, frequently calling the purchasing department for assistance in correctly entering the information.
9) Contact the five people in the approval chain to ask them to expedite approval (this step included leaving voice messages, initiating follow-up phone calls, and making personal visits).
10) After answering all questions regarding the purchase to all who were now involved, place the order with the designated vendor.

Upon receiving the projector three weeks later, he considered how difficult it was to place the order and how long it took to receive. He decided to check alternatives outside of corporate guidelines for ordering the projector. He found an electronics store on the internet, where the laptop projector he had ordered was available at half the price *including* overnight shipping. Bryant thought of the additional resources AirSPACE had used to procure the projector: staff who reviewed the order, entered financial and accounting information, reviewed and filed paperwork, and audited spending. With a little less energy and motivation, Bryant returned to his work.

In a Low-Friction Organization like a small start-up company, buying a laptop projector would be an insignificant event. Someone would simply order a projector on-line and use a credit card. They would receive the lowest price with next-day delivery. The process would be simple and efficient, like riding a brand new, well-oiled bicycle. The task would be accomplished quickly and efficiently with no energy lost.

In High-Friction Organizations, there are bureaucracies and structures that prevent work from occurring efficiently. Those bureaucracies do not need to impact business as negatively as they do in AirSPACE, but in High-Friction Organizations, time, effort, energy, and motivation which could be spent doing something productive are, instead, spent overcoming Organizational Friction. Energy is frequently wasted because it is dissipated by Friction.

Now that you understand the connection between physics and how High-Friction Organizations operate, here are formal definitions of Organizational Mechanics terms.

Organizational Mechanics – Definitions

Organizational Energy: The total amount of work energy available to an organization for creating products and services and for increasing profitability.

Organizational Energy is the total work potential available to an organization. It is determined by two factors: the *number* of employees within an organization and the *quality* of those employees. Some organizations say "Our employees are our greatest resource." That is truer than they may realize!

Think of Organizational Energy as the batteries for the organization. If you have four batteries to power your mp3 player, the total energy available to you for powering the device is contained within those batteries. Similarly, employees within an organization provide the batteries – the *energy* – for powering the organization. Like batteries, the Organizational Energy provided by employees represents the maximum amount of work that an organization can accomplish. If the organization wants to increase its Organizational Energy, it must hire more employees or improve their current employees. It must acquire more or higher quality batteries.

Organizational Energy is converted into one of four categories: Useful Work, Non-Useful Work, Heat, and Invisibility Pain.

Organizational Friction: The lack of alignment that exists when an organization *says* it wants something but *really* wants something else. Friction can be present in a person, a group of people, or in the organization's attitudes.

Friction exists when two uneven or rough surfaces contact each other during motion. Friction causes a system, whether it is a mechanical object or an organization, to work less effectively and efficiently. Of course, a certain amount of Friction can be necessary. If your bicycle is stuck in mud and has no friction between its tires and the ground, the wheel will just spin when you pedal. Similarly, an organization must have *some* Friction to operate. Organizations need an accounting system in which people maintain receipts and request approval for spending. While this uses energy and does not contribute directly to making better products and services, it enables the organization to perform necessary functions such as tracking spending, controlling cash flow, and producing financial reports.

Organizational Friction exists when the organization (or a person within it) says it wants something but it *really* wants something else. When there are unspoken goals and values, people within the organization become frustrated because actions and behaviors do not align with words. The mismatch between spoken and unspoken goals are the rough and uneven surfaces that unassuming people rub against and create Heat.

Friction can exist as **_Point Sources_**, which are individuals. Friction can also exist as **_Ambient Sources_**. Ambient Sources of Friction are larger scale processes and attitudes. For example:

- Groups within the organization, such as a large department.
- Prevailing attitudes within the organization, such as a negative attitude towards subordinates.
- Broken processes, such as a broken reward and recognition system.

If you wish to increase the size of your box, you must learn how to analyze Friction and understand what it indicates about what people *really* want.

Useful Work: Work performed that results in better products and services or increased profitability.

Organizational Energy can be converted into Useful Work. Useful Work is the work done by employees to develop, create, or improve what the organization offers to customers. You see the results of an organization's Useful Work in its products and services.

Non-Useful Work: Work performed within an organization that does not result in better products and services.

Organizational Energy can also be converted into Non-Useful Work. Non-Useful Work is the energy employees expend which does not contribute to developing, creating, or improving products and services. Some Non-Useful Work, like work required to keep records for financial reporting, is necessary for maintaining normal business operations and is related to the minimum required Friction described earlier. Non-Useful Work also represents the wasted energy employees expend through organizational inefficiencies, such as using outdated computer systems, following overly-bureaucratic processes, and doing 'busy-work.' Non-Useful Work also represents some darker sides of business. It is the work done by people with hidden agendas which do not support an organization's spoken goals. It is also the work done to build power, control, and territory. In High-Friction Organizations, a large amount of Organizational Energy is channeled into Non-Useful Work.

Heat: Wasted energy from interfacing inappropriately with the Friction in an organization.

Heat is created when someone interacts improperly with an organization's Friction. Heat is wasted energy, but it is more harmful than Non-Useful Work because the person who creates Heat feels negative effects. ***Heat results in pain for the individual creating the Heat***.

> ### High-Friction Organizations HATE HEAT.

Many people in organizations are Heat Creators. Heat Creators are prevalent because they are unaware of Friction's existence. They do not recognize the symptoms of Friction which they must navigate around to avoid creating Heat. Furthermore, people do not understand the negative impacts of creating Heat. Not only does the individual suffer because High-Friction Organizations punish those who create Heat, but the people around the Heat

Creator also feel the tension, aggravation, and wasted energy. If people understood the effects of creating Heat, most would avoid doing so.

> **Creating Heat in a High-Friction Organization will keep you from getting what you *really* want.**

You must understand what Heat is **not**. Heat is *not* generated when you challenge people within an organization. It is generated when you challenge them *inappropriately*. Heat is not generated when you assert your ideas within an organization. It is generated when you assert your ideas *inappropriately*. SPACE is about managing your *interface* with your organization. To be successful, you must understand *how* to challenge someone and assert your ideas *appropriately*. Note that your organization determines what *is* and *is not* appropriate.

Invisibility Pain: Energy used to control frustration and maintain composure in the midst of Friction and Non-Useful Work. Invisibility Pain, also called the "Low Level of Pain," is less harmful to individuals than Heat.

Invisibility Pain is an energy expenditure by an individual when they perceive their organization doing something inappropriate or senseless. People experience Invisibility Pain when they know that the proper course of action is to take a deep breath, shake their head, smile, and continue their day.

Working in a High-Friction Organization is not ideal. Employees must *optimize* this non-ideal situation to work most effectively. This requires acceptance that things will never be perfect. In extreme situations, it requires acceptance that some things are sadly broken. This acceptance uses an individual's energy in the form of Invisibility Pain. Invisibility Pain is the constant Low-Level of Pain you feel when you accept the fact that the physics of your organization makes you less efficient and effective than you could otherwise be. You feel this pain, for example, when you know you are doing Non-Useful Work to manage your interface properly.

High-Friction Organization: An organization that, because of its high level of Friction, significantly reduces its employees' effectiveness. Employees' energy is often wasted as Non-Useful Work, Heat, and Invisibility Pain.

At the extreme, a High-Friction Organization is a dysfunctional organization which hampers the efforts of the most dedicated and motivated employees to do their jobs. These organizations are highly political and unfriendly, especially at lower levels. An enormous amount of Non-Useful Work is performed as employees spend their energy on combating bureaucracies and other non-value-added activities instead of focusing on the organization's greater good. Heat is often created as employees constantly rub against Friction.

A key characteristic of High-Friction Organizations is that they value behaviors over results. High-Friction Organizations would rather their employees act in certain ways than achieve a positive result. High-Friction Organizations prefer that their workers fail while behaving according to organizational rules rather than succeed while behaving outside of organizational norms.

High-Friction Organizations are especially difficult environments for employees who strive to 'do the right thing.' These organizations *really* want something other than what they *say* they want. Because 'do-the-right-thing' employees focus on the organization's stated mission instead of the organization's *true* goals, they feel unappreciated and unrewarded because their loyalty and dedication is not valued or rewarded.

The Heart of Organizational Mechanics: The Law of Conversation of Organizational Energy

The Law of Conservation of Organizational Energy ties together the definitions of Organizational Mechanics into an easy-to-understand explanation of why Useful Work is so difficult to perform in High-Friction Organizations. It shows how the Organizational Energy of employees is converted to Useful Work, Non-Useful Work, Heat, and Invisibility Pain.

> **The Law of Conservation of Organizational Energy:** Organizational Energy is neither created nor destroyed; its form is only changed from one form of energy into another.

The Law of Conservation of Organizational Energy is an equation, so the quantities on both sides will always be equal. The left side of the equation shows a pie representing the total Organizational Energy available for making great products and services. The right side of the equation shows the four ca`tegories into which Organizational Energy can be converted: Useful Work,

Non-Useful Work, Heat, and Invisibility Pain. The equation starts with equal Organizational Energy pies on each side.

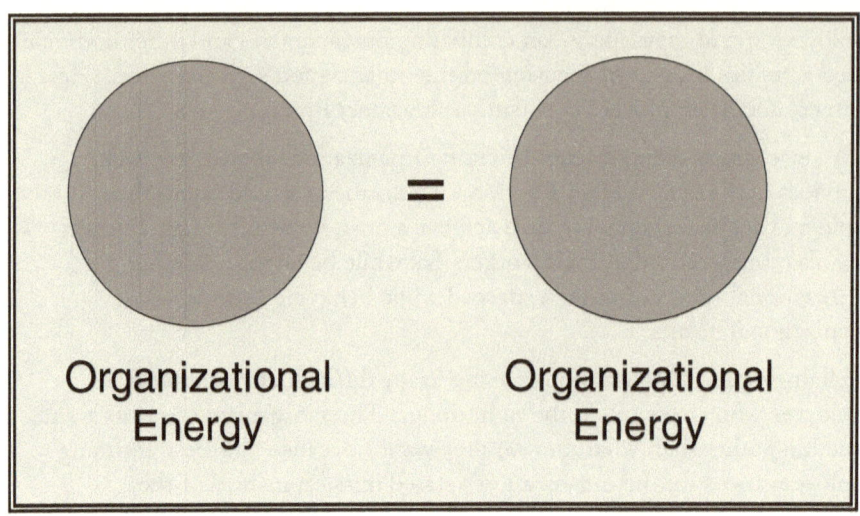

Setting the Equality for the Law of Conservation of Organizational Energy

Each day, employees expend their energy in various ways. They perform a certain amount of Useful Work and Non-Useful Work, create some Heat, and expend energy in Invisibility Pain as represented below:

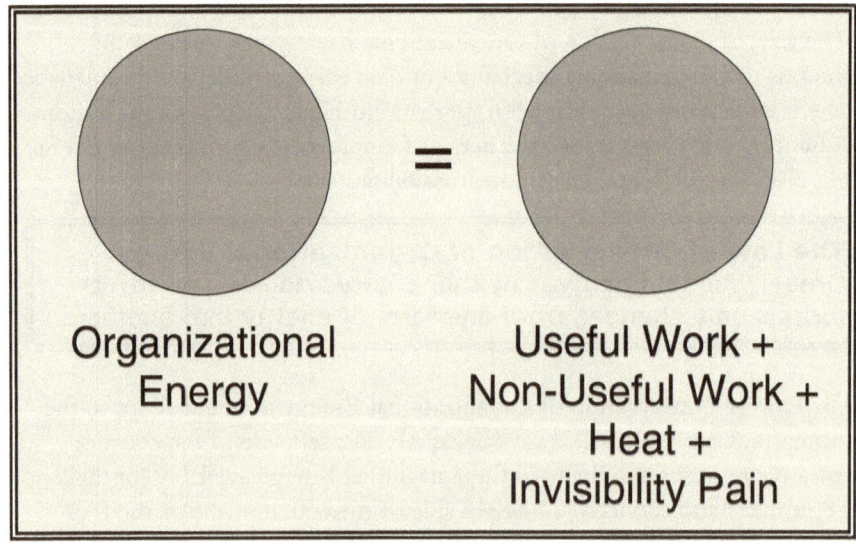

The Forms into which Organizational Energy can be Converted

In the example below, 75% of employees' energy is converted into Useful Work. That is, three quarters of an employees' energy is devoted to work that results in better and more useful products or services for the organization's customers.

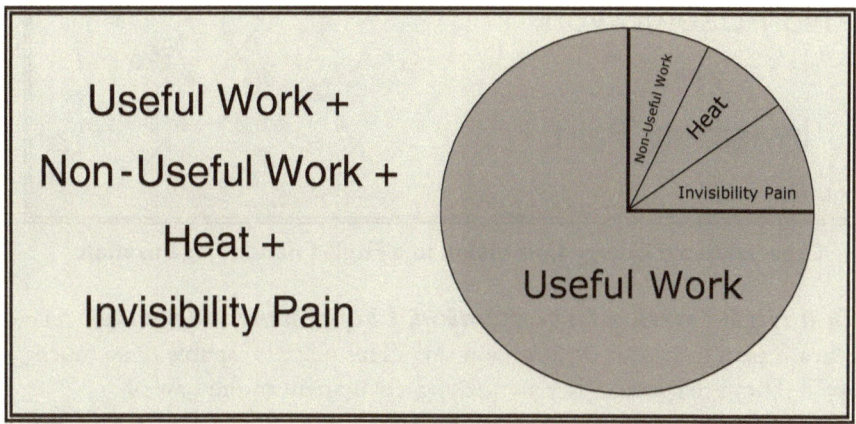

One Example of the Proportions of Organizational Energy Conversion

As Friction increases, Organizational Energy is channeled in different quantities to Useful Work, Non-Useful Work, Heat, and Invisibility Pain. Employees create more Heat simply because more Friction is present. Non-Useful Work increases as people expend their energy working through excessive bureaucracies and other non-value-added pursuits. Some employees understand Organizational Mechanics so the amount of Invisibility Pain those employees feel increases. These factors significantly reduce the amount of Useful Work accomplished.

Because the size of the pie representing Organizational Energy is constant and cannot change, only the size of the slices can change. If Non-Useful Work, Heat, and Invisibility Pain increases, what *must* happen to Useful Work? It **must** decrease!

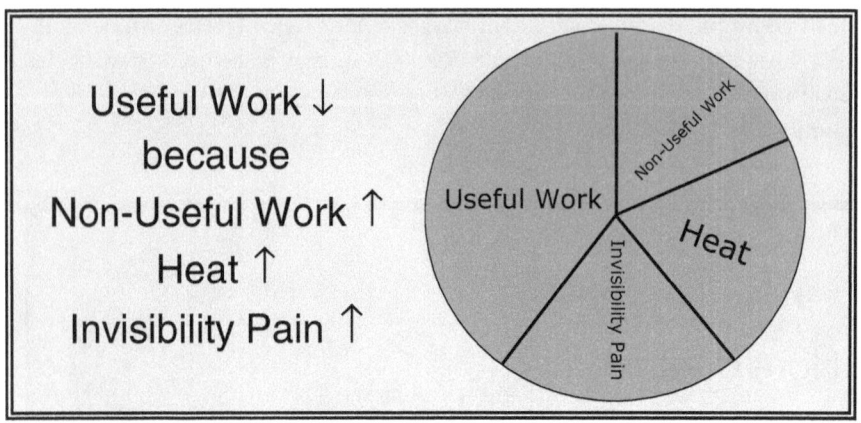

Useful Work ↓
because
Non-Useful Work ↑
Heat ↑
Invisibility Pain ↑

Organizational Energy Conversion in a High-Friction Organization

In a High-Friction Organization, Useful Work decreases. Have you heard people in your organization say: "This place is capable of so much more"? They are correct; they are making a statement of the Law of Conservation of Organizational Energy. This Law explains why an organization can never work as smoothly as its employees wish it would.

The Law of Conservation of Organizational Energy shows that Useful Work in a High-Friction Organization is reduced. You simply *will not* be able to accomplish as much as you believe you should.

Expecting to accomplish an impossible amount of Useful Work within your organization is like expecting something to happen against the laws of physics. It would be the same as expecting to throw a ball a mile or to jump 100 feet into the air. *Don't be frustrated by physics!* You would never be upset at how slowly a ball drops to the ground. Physics determines the speed at which a ball drops and it would be silly to scream at the ball to drop faster. Why become upset about something that is acting according to the laws of physics and is, therefore, entirely out of your control? Organizational Mechanics explains why you cannot accomplish the work in a High-Friction Organization which you believe you *should*. Many people are frustrated that they cannot do their job because so much Non-Useful Work gets in the way. They complain about how much energy they waste. Yet complaining about how little work gets done is as useful as complaining about how slowly a ball drops to the ground. It's just physics. When you realize that your organization's basic structure makes it impossible to efficiently convert Organizational Energy into Useful Work, you can begin to release your frustration at how little Useful Work you can do.

Example: **AirSPACE**

The Law of Conservation of Organizational Energy

Joelle	**Jeffrey**	**Darren**
Supervisor	Engineer	Supplier Liaison

An AirSPACE engineer effectively used the Law of Conservation of Organizational Energy to resolve a problem without creating Heat. Defectco Inc., one of AirSPACE's suppliers, constantly shipped defective engine parts into AirSPACE's Engine Manufacturing Facility. As a result, many engines failed their certification tests after they were built. Defectco's parts were made so poorly that they would frequently not fit into engines during assembly. The defective parts began to cost AirSPACE a significant amount of wasted time and money.

Joelle was the production manager responsible for ensuring that high quality engines were built on time and within budget. Joelle was frustrated that Defectco's poor quality was harming her performance. When her engines failed their certification tests, Joelle's team was forced to disassemble engines and make costly repairs. When defective parts did not fit in the engine, Joelle's assembly lines shut down, bringing engine production to a halt. One morning, after a particularly bad batch of Defecto's parts, she called Jeffrey, the engineer who supported her assembly lines. Frustrated, she demanded that Jeffrey ensure that her quality problems were fixed.

Jeffrey knew about SPACE and avoided Heat Creation at work. He did what he could to give people what they *really* wanted. He understood the Law of Conservation of Organizational Energy and recognized that things happen slowly in High-Friction Organizations like AirSPACE. When he approached problems, he worked hard to develop solutions which were organizationally friendly, channeled the most energy to Useful Work, and channeled the least energy to Heat.

Jeffrey also knew why Defectco's quality problems had been overlooked for so long. Darren was the quality manager responsible for ensuring that suppliers delivered high-quality parts. It was Darren's job to guarantee that Defectco's parts did not cause problems for Joelle. Joelle should have gone to Darren to resolve the issues and Jeffrey found it interesting that Joelle would come to him instead. Unfortunately, Jeffrey knew it was now incumbent upon him to find a solution.

Joelle's problems persisted largely because of Darren's relationship with Defectco. Darren had a good relationship with the supplier, perhaps too good. Defectco frequently took him to lunches, sporting events, and golf outings. Darren tried to work with Defectco to improve their quality but was overly patient with their slow progress. Jeffrey recognized that he would not be able to address Darren's relationship with Defectco at his own level within the organization's hierarchy. He concluded that he must work within the constraints of that relationship.

Jeffrey knew that Defectco's performance was causing Joelle such a headache that she was ready to bring the problem to AirSPACE's higher management. He also recognized that if she did escalate the problem, she would create a lot of Heat. AirSPACE's management would cause pain for everyone involved through constant status reviews and additional assignments. Darren would be angry with Joelle and would be reluctant to help her in other areas. Darren's management would also resent Joelle and be more resistant to helping her when other problems arose. Jeffrey first needed to persuade Joelle that tangible actions were being taken to resolve the problem so she would not escalate it.

Jeffrey understood the Law of Conservation of Organizational Energy. He recognized the Friction in the current situation, which included close relationships with suppliers, protectiveness of territory, and an aversion to involving upper management in problems. He recognized that, as a result, more of his energy will be converted into Non-Useful Work. He ultimately wanted to ensure that his energy was not channeled into Heat. This was really Joelle's and Darren's problem; he was caught in the middle. In AirSPACE's High-Friction environment, Jeffrey recognized this as an opportunity for Darren and Joelle to focus their blame and frustration on him.

Finally, Jeffrey understood a key distinction between his drive to improve AirSPACE and the realities of its organizational structure. Regardless of Darren's relationship with Defectco, if Jeffrey did not prevent an internal organizational fight from occurring, everyone would lose. Due to AirSPACE's organizational structure (which Jeffrey was powerless to change at that moment), an internal fight would not solve the current problem any faster and would lead to bad feelings and sour relationships that would damage future problem-solving efforts. Jeffrey recognized that, with his knowledge of SPACE and of the people involved in this situation, he was in a perfect position to bridge the communication gap between Darren and Joelle.

Jeffrey said to Joelle: "I will work to make sure that your problems with Defectco go away. I need some help to make that happen. We don't have any data on how many defects Defectco sends in. And we don't have any specific data on how much time and money we are losing. We're not really sure where to start addressing this problem. Can we develop a data collection plan?" Joelle said: "What's the point of all of this? You *know* Darren's not going to get any action out of Defectco." Jeffrey answered: "I know, Joelle. But before we tell Darren's boss that we have a big problem, let's just collect some data so we can be specific about what is happening."

Joelle agreed to work with Jeffrey to develop the plan and assign responsibility for who would collect the information. Jeffrey said: "I will review this quality data with Darren every Friday. We'll review the prior week's data and list the largest problems. We will then meet with Defectco every Tuesday to review their work plans. Give us a month. If you don't see any action, then I don't blame you for taking this data to our management and showing that Darren isn't doing his job."

Again, Joelle agreed with Jeffrey's plan. She felt that Jeffrey was working for her and that she was being well taken care of. She believed her problems from Defectco would soon go away. Jeffrey had successfully given Joelle what she *really* wanted. Now he needed to implement the second half of his plan: to convince Darren to force Defectco into action.

Jeffrey met with Darren and said: "Darren, I learned that Joelle's area has been losing a lot of production time and money lately. They've been doing a lot of expensive repairs because of Defectco's bad parts. Joelle is collecting data about the problems they've had – she was totally ready to bring everything to our management. Last time she did that, it was such a mess for you and me and everyone else and I don't want to go through that again. Joelle has agreed not to escalate this issue yet. I think we have a month, but Joelle needs to see some improvements by that time. I need your help to make sure Defectco works with us on this."

Jeffrey presented the problem to Darren in a way that gave Darren what he *really* wanted. Darren could now avoid the perception that he was the cause of increasing the pressure on Defectco since Joelle and Jeffrey, not he, were collecting data on Defectco's quality. Darren could show that he was just trying to protect Defectco. Darren was now willing to help Jeffrey and Joelle because he believed his close relationship with Defectco was preserved.

Jeffrey was satisfied with the solution. He did not expect to fix AirSPACE's problems with Defectco in a day or even in a week. In Lower-Friction Organizations, they may have been able to fix the problems sooner. But in AirSPACE, he accepted the one-month timing plan as the price of High-Friction. Most importantly, he averted a showdown between Joelle's group and Darren's group, which could have caused long-lasting problems within the Engine Manufacturing Facility. He avoided the creation of Heat. By accepting the additional Non-Useful Work to avoid rubbing against Organizational Friction, Jeffrey found the optimal solution to Defectco's quality problems in AirSPACE's High Friction environment.

The key points from the Law of Conservation of Organizational Energy are:

- In any organization, there is a finite amount of Organizational Energy.
- Because of its structure, an organization can only achieve a finite amount of Useful Work.
- As Friction increases, employees will spend more time doing Non-Useful Work.
- As Friction increases, more people will create Heat.
- As Heat and Non-Useful Work increase, Useful Work accomplished by the organization **must** decrease.

The Law of Conservation of Organization Energy explains how much work can be accomplished within an organization. A High-Friction Organization simply cannot produce as much Useful Work as a Lower-Friction Organization. Many people want their organization to perform better and *know* it could if it operated differently. Unfortunately, an organization, like an individual, is built and structured with certain capabilities. Those capabilities determine how much Useful Work an organization can produce. The existence of Friction simply reduces an organization's efficiency and effectiveness. Being frustrated about this is like being frustrated by physics. *Don't be frustrated by physics!*

Friction is the Organization's Problem; Heat is *Your* Problem

You, not your organization, will be negatively impacted by the Heat you create. High-Friction Organizations are accustomed to Heat; they expect it to be created. Over time, they build structures and processes to deal with those who create Heat. They marginalize Heat Creators, placing them in areas where they cannot do much damage or wearing them down until they leave or become resigned to their place within the organization. Individuals are powerless against the organization's mechanisms for managing Heat. In the face of Heat, the organization will continue moving along its path without interruption, like a locomotive. As a result, individuals who create Heat will feel the full pain from the organization's mechanisms for dealing with Heat Creators.

Does the presence of organizational Friction mean that Heat Creation is unavoidable? Absolutely not. When you work in a High-Friction Organization, you are not condemned to a small box. Refer to the earlier bicycle analogy. If your bicycle has a rusty front wheel, can you ride it without creating Heat? Of course you can, if you think creatively. One way to do this is to ride a wheelie. When the front wheel does not turn, Heat is not created. Of course, riding a wheelie is not easy at first; it takes patience to learn and practice to perfect. It takes *finesse*. In a High-Friction Organization, you must work in a particular way to avoid creating Heat. You must practice behaviors that avoid creating Heat just as you would need to practice riding a wheelie. You will become more skilled over time and, while it takes a bit more balance and finesse, you will no longer create Heat.

Those who are successful in High-Friction Organizations recognize that the path to success is to manage their interface in a way that does not create Heat. Organizational Mechanics shows you how to tune your interface. If you are frustrated because of your organization's inefficiencies, you will act out of that frustration in various ways. Those frustrations will lead to Heat Creation, which will keep you from getting what you *really* want. The first step to properly tuning your interface is to recognize and accept the physics of your organization. In a High-Friction Organization, you must modify your expectations regarding the amount of Useful Work that can be accomplished. *This does not mean you should stop working hard for improvements within your organization.* This *does* suggest that you must consider the physics of your organization when choosing where to focus your energy and when setting your expectations of the results you can achieve. When you modify your expectations of how work is accomplished, you will feel less frustrated. In addition to doing your work in a way that is friendlier to your organization, you will channel more of your energy to Useful Work since you will no longer create Heat. You will accomplish more work, get better results, and feel more peace because of your new expectations.

Individuals choose their behaviors. Each day, they decide whether they will rub against the organization's Friction and create Heat. Just because there is Friction in your organization does not mean you will create Heat. Your success in a High-Friction Organization is determined by how effectively you avoid creating Heat. You can choose an interface that, in spite of the Friction around you, enables you to work in a way your organization appreciates. The proper interface will undoubtedly require practice, effort, and finesse, but it respects and accepts the physics regarding how work can be accomplished within your High-Friction Organization. You will be rewarded for your additional time and effort with a larger box and more freedom to do what you believe is important. You can choose to turn the rusty front wheel or you can choose to ride the wheelie. Friction is the organization's problem; Heat is *your* problem.

> To be successful in a High-Friction Organization, you must constantly focus on your interface to ensure that you work and behave in ways appreciated by your organization.

Survey - Conclusions

Because SPACE is a behavior-based approach, it focuses on your *behaviors* within your organization and not your ideas. You can have the best ideas, but if your method of delivering them is not acceptable to your organization, you will not be able to turn those great ideas into reality. Friction has implications for how you supply ideas, challenge management, and make positive change. *How* you make positive change can be more important in a High-Friction Organization than the change you are trying to make.

SPACE begins by Surveying your organization to understand how much Friction is present. Because of Friction, the amount of Useful Work you can expect to accomplish is lower, as shown by the Law of Conservation of Organizational Energy. Organizational Mechanics is as much a fact of life as the speed at which a ball falls to the ground. When you understand Organizational Mechanics and accept the physics, you can begin to let go of the frustration that causes you to create Heat and shrink your box. With your larger box, you will have more flexibility and greater autonomy. More of your energy will be converted into Useful Work for your organization.

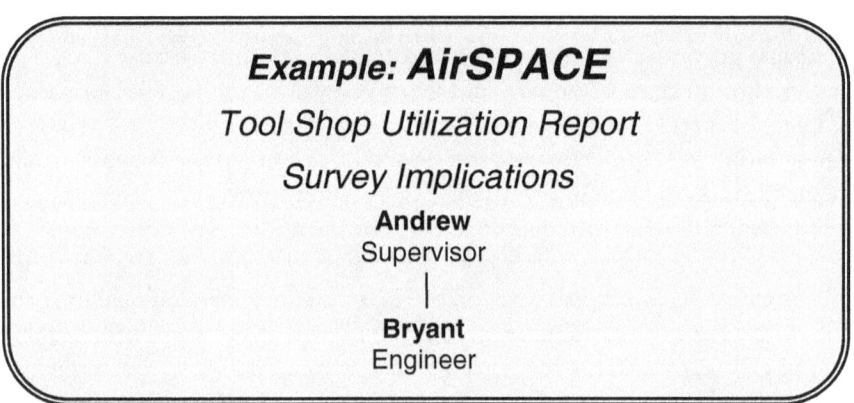

Example: **AirSPACE**

Tool Shop Utilization Report

Survey Implications

Andrew
Supervisor

|

Bryant
Engineer

Bryant was asked to put together a one-page report showing how effectively the AirSPACE Tool Shop was being used. His supervisor just asked him in a public department meeting to create something different: a one-page report with numbers that "look good." From a SPACE perspective, what should Bryant do?

Bryant Surveyed his organization. He reviewed the list of Symptoms of High-Friction Organizations and found that AirSPACE exhibits 12 of the 14 symptoms. He is definitely in a High-Friction Organization. Thus, AirSPACE accepts that a large amount of its employees' Organizational Energy will be converted into Non-Useful Work and Heat. *How* he does his job may be more important than doing a good job. Bryant is not happy about that, but he recognizes and reluctantly accepts the physics of AirSPACE's organization.

Bryant knows his one-page report could help someone manage the Tool Shop effectively. He also knows that a report which treads around the problem will not achieve the same goal as quickly. Bryant understands that with a larger box, he will have more freedom and flexibility in the future to make a positive difference. He knows that this one-page report will not be his only opportunity to do great things for AirSPACE.

At this point, Bryant is weighing the short-term consideration of creating Heat versus the long-term consideration of finding or creating greater opportunities to make improvements. In the short term, Heat will hurt Bryant and keep him from getting what he *really* wants. In the long term, however, many possibilities exist. So, while Bryant considers changing the report as Andrew asked him to, he needs more tools to guide his decision.

Key Points from Survey:

1) Only a certain amount of Useful Work can be accomplished in a High-Friction Organization.

2) The higher the Friction in your organization, the less Useful Work will be accomplished.

3) *DON'T BE FRUSTRATED BY PHYSICS!*

4) Be aware of the Friction in your organization so you can avoid rubbing up against that Friction and creating Heat.

5) Because "your organization" can refer to many different workgroups, perform frequent Surveys to help you tune your interface on-the-fly.

6) Friction is the organization's problem – Heat is your problem.

7) Creating Heat will cause you pain and keep you from getting what you *really* want.

8) Tune your interface so your *behaviors* are acceptable to your organization. You cannot turn your great ideas into reality unless your organization accepts and values the way you work and behave.

If you want positive change in your organization, you must change your interface. Fortunately, you have full control over your interface. You will be successful if you tune your interface to meet the following goal: **work to give your organization what it *really* wants**. The next step in SPACE is to tune your interface to focus on giving your organization what it *really* wants so you can increase the size of your box and get what you *really* want.

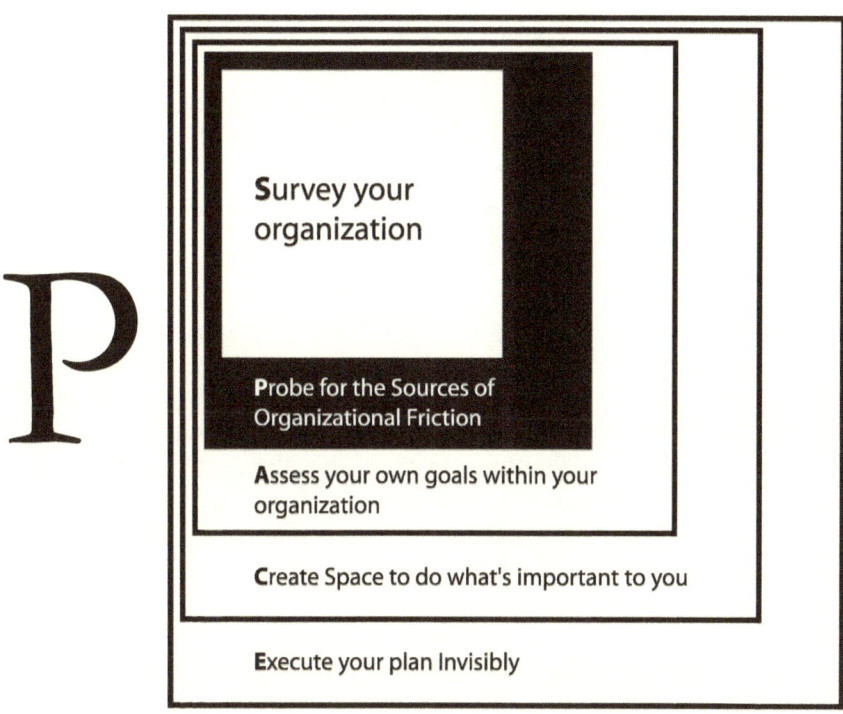

Survey your organization

Probe for the Sources of Organizational Friction

Assess your own goals within your organization

Create Space to do what's important to you

Execute your plan Invisibly

P

While Friction causes so much wasted energy and frustration, it is useful for determining what organizations *really* want. Because Friction is a disconnect between what people say they want and what they *really* want, it shows you where to Probe deeper to understand your organization's true goals. When you work for the greater good of your organization, actions that work against that greater good will stand out and catch your attention. Friction reveals itself during times when you perceive that something is not quite right. When you are confused, surprised, or frustrated, look carefully for the presence of a Source of Friction.

You can use Friction to learn what your organization *really* wants simply by **observing behaviors**. A person's or an organization's behavior, over time, is a reliable indicator of what they *really* want. When you observe a behavior in a single situation, it may not reveal someone's true goals. However, over time, when you see consistent patterns of behaviors, you can rely on that observed information more than the information you hear.

Probe will show you how to use Friction in your organization to determine what your organization *really* wants. The Probe chapter will:

- Explain how Friction develops in organizations and why it stays.

- Show you how observing behaviors is the key to understanding what organizations and people within them *really* want.
- Understand the two main Sources of Friction: Ambient and Point Sources.
- Discuss three Ambient Sources of Friction in detail so you will begin to recognize Friction and sharpen your ability to interpret unspoken goals.
- Show you how frustrating situations can be used as learning experiences for understanding what others *really* want.

Probe turns Friction into an opportunity for actionable learning. Probe shows you how to identify Friction, then determine what it reveals about what your organization *really* wants. When you observe others' behaviors and your organization's reaction to them, you can uncover what your organization rewards and appreciates. If you approach your job with an interface that your organization does not appreciate, it will resist your efforts. If you approach your job with behaviors your organization values, it will reward you with a bigger box and the benefits that come with it.

Friction: What it Is and What it Does

Recall the definition of Organizational Friction:

> **Organizational Friction**: The lack of alignment that exists when an organization *says* it wants something but *really* wants something else. Friction can be present in a person, a group of people, or in the organization's attitudes.

Where does Organizational Friction come from? Just as new bicycles do not have rusty parts with friction, organizations do not have Friction when they form. Over time, bicycles and organizations can slowly develop Friction due to lack of attention to care and maintenance. Friction affects everything within the organization, including how departments are arranged, the system for advancement and promotion, and how employees prepare for reviews with their management. To illustrate how Friction develops and changes an organization, consider NewOrg, Inc., an organization formed to make mp3 players.

In the beginning, all members of NewOrg share a common goal to deliver an mp3 player which customers love. Everyone works together to do whatever is necessary to deliver their product to their customers. In NewOrg's small organization, engineers do accounting and marketing work as required to facilitate the business. Everyone understands that anything which does not support development and delivery of great mp3 players is not useful to

NewOrg's end goal. If NewOrg does not efficiently and effectively perform its work, it will not survive in the market.

After NewOrg's initial success, it will expand to increase profits. NewOrg will hire more people and will, eventually, hire specialists. They will hire an accounting staff to focus on accounting. They will hire a marketing staff to determine the best marketing strategy for NewOrg's expanding product line. Specialists provide great efficiencies for the organization. Accountants are best suited to do accounting work; they are trained to perform accounting tasks effectively and efficiently. An accounting staff will free NewOrg's engineers to focus on engineering, the job for which they have been effectively trained. With specialization, NewOrg's members will focus on the jobs for which their skills are best suited.

While specialization provides a variety of benefits, it also generates various costs. Specialists can become focused on their particular function and lose sight of the organization's overall objectives. Specialists are often measured in ways to drive them to focus intensely on their explicit responsibilities, causing them to focus on their tasks as their end goal. Accountants may become so focused on maintaining paperwork and following procedures that they unnecessarily slow the pace of business. Engineers may focus on building product features which they believe are fresh and exciting but customers do not want. Marketers may promise dates and quantities for product delivery that the manufacturing department could never meet.

What happens when Marketing makes product delivery promises without consulting Manufacturing? Animosity will develop between the two functions. Manufacturing will voice their frustrations about Marketing, such as: "they have their heads in the clouds!" Marketing will voice their frustrations about Manufacturing, for example: "can they deliver *any* product to our customers on time?" Over time, jokes and griping will turn into enmity, resulting in less collaboration and communication. This leads to the development of hard divisions between groups that do nothing to benefit NewOrg's customers. More Heat is now generated within the organization, leaving less energy available for Useful Work.

As a result of specialization, NewOrg's overall goal of producing mp3 players has now changed for its members, and those narrower goals may not be openly discussed. While the accounting department *says* it wants to support the creation of great mp3 players, it may *really* want to focus on tracking and managing cash flows. Manufacturing may *say* they want to produce high quality products but, when they are measured on *how much* they produce, they may *really* just want their production lines to keep running. These unspoken goals, which are different from NewOrg's spoken goals, are the Friction in the organization.

Friction now exists because the actions and behaviors of NewOrg's members are working against each other and against the organization's overall goal.

As you learn about Friction, recognize that it is unsavory, resulting in unpleasant truths of how organizations operate. Friction changes how Organizational Energy is converted, reducing the amount of Useful Work you can accomplish. While frustrating, this reality is the physics of a High-Friction Organization, and becoming frustrated by physics is as useful as being frustrated by how fast a ball drops to the ground. *Friction, however, is useful for understanding motivations and expectations.* When you understand those unsavory aspects of Friction, you will be equipped to navigate around it and avoid creating Heat, which will shrink your box and keep you from getting what you *really* want. As you learn about Friction, recognize the implications that will help you to create a successful interface with your organization.

Two Types of Friction: Ambient and Point Sources

Friction manifests on two levels within organizations. On a macro level, Friction creates general attitudes which pervade the organization and results in the establishment of inefficient departments and processes. On a micro level, Friction allows individual employees to work in ways that are not in the organization's best interests.

Ambient Sources of Friction exist on a large scale within an organization. They represent overall organizational attitudes vis-à-vis the attitudes of individuals. Some examples of Friction's manifestations on an organizational level are: overly bureaucratic processes, chimneys or silos (areas that operate as if they were entirely separate from the rest of the organization), and a prevailing negative attitude towards subordinates. *Ambient Sources of Friction reveal what the organization really wants independent of what individuals really want.*

Point Sources of Friction are people whose goals are contrary to the organization's overall goals. While they may be difficult or maddening to work with, Point Sources usually have a specific set of objectives and expectations that effectively explain their frustrating behavior. *Point Sources of Friction reveal what an individual really wants independent of what the organization really wants.*

Ambient Sources of Friction

Ambient Sources of Friction reflect the culture of an organization and tell you which behaviors it finds acceptable. You use your knowledge of Ambient Sources when you enter an unfamiliar area within your organization. If your job requires you to meet with someone outside of your immediate work group, knowledge of Ambient Sources guides you on how to behave without creating Heat.

Some examples of Ambient Sources of Friction are:

- Overly bureaucratic processes
- Functional chimneys or silos
- Negative attitudes toward subordinates
- Processes for rewards and promotion that value behavior over results
- A severe vertical hierarchy (i.e. you must get permission from many different levels of management to make decisions)

Every Source of Friction develops within an organization for a specific reason and persists due to lack of attention to its negative effects. Through examples of Ambient Sources, you will see how you can match their existence to what an organization *really* wants, enabling you to determine how to give your organization what it *really* wants.

Ambient Source #1: Bureaucratic Processes

When you think of the word "bureaucracy," you may think of words like "waste," "inaction," and "frustration." Bureaucracies, however, can serve a useful purpose. Consider a purchasing department, a critical part of any large organization. A purchasing department helps the organization maintain the necessary cash flow to keep operations moving along smoothly. A purchasing department keeps records for financial reporting. It develops economies of scale by placing bulk supply orders for the organization instead of leaving each individual area to negotiate a better price for lower-volume purchases. Finally, a purchasing department helps employees play to their strengths. Engineers should not spend time making purchases for small items and managing the associated record keeping. They should be engineering, and letting people who are skilled at purchasing manage that function. Bureaucracies perform tasks that may not be pivotal in creating better products and services. They do, however, provide the minimum level of Friction required to give the organization traction in executing its business.

Problems arise when a bureaucratic process begins to do more than simply facilitate the process for which it was developed. These problems develop as a result of how the bureaucracy's performance is assessed. A purchasing department which is measured on the amount of money the organization spends may always pursue the lowest-cost options, regardless of the quality of the items purchased. While this is a natural reaction to how they are measured, it drives them to exhibit inefficient behaviors to meet their own internal objectives rather than focus on the overall organization.

When a bureaucracy begins to focus on its own internal objectives, it becomes a Source of Friction. It no longer wants what the organization *says* it wants. When you work with the bureaucracy, you must recognize the Friction. Instead of assuming that the bureaucracy wants to support the overall business, you must recognize that the bureaucracy is driven to meet some other objective. You must not be surprised and frustrated when the bureaucracy does not act in the organization's best interests. If you wish to get what you want from a bureaucracy, you must understand what it wants and recognize when you are working against those objectives. What, then, do bureaucratic processes *really* want? You discover this by observing behaviors.

Observing behaviors can tell you what a bureaucracy *doesn't* really want. If a bureaucracy consistently takes a long time to respond to requests, it does not value speed and efficiency. Such a bureaucracy would constantly generate complaints. Everyone in the organization would know about the delays caused by the bureaucracy. The continued existence of the delays indicates that the organization is not driven to solve the problem. When you observe consistent patterns of behavior, you receive clues about what a bureaucracy *really* wants.

When a bureaucratic process is a Source of Friction, it works to achieve one or more of the following:

- Justify its existence
- Defend its own territory
- Exert power and control for those within and outside of the process
- Provide the ability to give and deflect blame
- Maintain the status quo

Bureaucratic processes may be seen as one of the first areas to be downsized when the organization experiences financial difficulty. The bureaucracy may attempt to emphasize its legitimacy to deflect cuts. The department may believe that if it increases in size, it will be perceived as too important to eliminate. Because bureaucratic processes are established to facilitate business, they are a source of power and control for someone who knows how to use it as such. A bureaucratic process may help others give and deflect blame because their complex processes mask transactions, making it difficult to clarify facts when something goes wrong. Finally, when an overly-bureaucratic process maintains the status quo, they avoid the difficult change required to increase their efficiency and effectiveness.

While it is unpleasant to accept that entities within your own organization *really* want the things listed above, remember that this list applies to bureaucratic processes that have grown into Sources of Friction. They have been neglected or allowed to transform into an entity that is incompatible with the organization's overall goals. You must avoid creating Heat when working with these processes. You will successfully get what you need from the process and will ultimately waste less energy if you do not resist the Friction and create Heat.

Remember: not all bureaucratic processes are bad; they serve a necessary function in most organizations. However, if a bureaucratic process has developed into a Source of Friction, it is, by definition, working towards goals that are different than the stated goals of the organization. You must be aware of Sources of Friction and what they *really* want so you can avoid creating Heat.

Ambient Source #2: Functional Chimneys or Silos

Some organizations have departments or groups that operate as if they were an individual company instead of a team within their larger organization. It is as if the department was a chimney within an organization that has many such chimneys. Because these chimneys are rigid and immovable, they do not generate synergies with other departments. There is very little sharing of information. A "functional chimney" or "silo" describes a department that stands alone, by itself, without recognition that it is a part of a larger system.

Functional chimneys develop innocently within organizations. Centralized departments, the precursor to functional chimneys, provided a central place for an organization's core knowledge. If there were a centralized marketing department, all important marketing information could be found there. The organization's marketing experts were also there, so anyone looking for marketing information knew exactly where to go. Because the experts were in one small area, they all worked together and learned together, increasing their effectiveness over time. Finally, a centralized department promoted esprit de corps among its members, enabling those employees to feel at home and comfortable with those around them.

Over time and without appropriate attention, centralized departments can harden into functional chimneys. This happens for many of the same reasons that inefficient bureaucracies form: people become focused on their individual function at the expense of the overall organization.

The large American automotive companies provide relevant examples of the downsides of functional chimneys. Those companies have product development and manufacturing organizations. Their respective roles are straightforward: Product Development creates the design for a vehicle, while Manufacturing must build the design that Product Development creates. Ideally, to minimize costs and maximize quality, Product Development and

Manufacturing would frequently talk to each other as the design is created. Manufacturing would understand which designs could be easily built with high quality, and which designs could not. Tight linkage between Product Development and Manufacturing throughout the design process would minimize costly changes as Manufacturing prepares to build the design. In reality, however, Product Development and Manufacturing act as functional chimneys. Designs are "thrown over the wall" for Manufacturing to figure out how to build. Each organization acts as a "territory" or a "turf" and there is a very clear boundary between them. This results in costly late changes to manufacturing equipment and vehicle designs. It can cost millions of dollars to change an automobile when it cannot be manufactured effectively.

As before, when a functional chimney is a Source of Friction, it works to achieve one or more of the following:

- Justify its existence
- Defend its own territory
- Exert power and control for those within and outside of the process
- Provide the ability to give and deflect blame
- Maintain the status quo

A chimney is resistant to interference from outsiders. It believes there is safety in numbers, so a strong chimney is difficult to dismantle or penetrate. Due to its strength, it is more successful in imposing its will within the organization. When problems occur, a chimney can claim that the problems were someone else's fault. Finally, because a chimney is inherently inefficient, organizational improvements threaten its existence and territory.

Ambient Source #3: Negative attitude towards Subordinates

In some organizations, it is clear who is at the top of the hierarchy and who is at the bottom. Some organizations have a clear and tangible negative attitude towards subordinates. That is, if you are lower within your organization's hierarchy, you and your job function is valued *less* than someone who is higher in the hierarchy.

The military provides a readily accessible stereotype for an organization with a negative attitude towards subordinates. You can picture a Sergeant screaming into a soldier's face: "You're worthless! Drop and give me 200 pushups!" Why does the military allow and encourage its members of higher rank to be so sharp with their subordinates? Lower-ranked members in the military must be well trained for a single purpose: to follow commands. In the heat of a battle, there is no room for collaboration or questioning orders. Soldiers must hear and obey immediately. Officers cannot accept differing ideas or opinions; they need specific and immediate action.

This approach is not appropriate for most other organizations. Organizations working to make great products and services must maximize the value they receive from their employees. They must unleash their employees' creativity, ingenuity, and productivity. A negative attitude towards subordinates stifles those qualities.

The negative attitude towards subordinates manifests itself in many ways. A visible sign of this is the size and layout of employees' offices. When eBay was a small and successful start-up company, the eBay CEO had a cubicle as her office, just like her subordinates[1]. eBay needed their lower-level employees to understand that they were as important to the company as upper management. Seeing the CEO in a cubicle was a clear sign that eBay's senior management viewed everyone in the company as vital to its success. Organizations do not *need* to provide managers with spacious offices and nice furniture while subordinates have cubicles and old desks. They *choose* to provide those contrasting accommodations.

Another visible sign of a negative attitude towards subordinates is a reserved parking space. Picture this: You walk into work on a windy winter morning. You were delayed coming to work, so you were forced to park at the back of the parking lot. You are now late for a meeting and are even later because you parked so far from the entrance to the office. As you hurry into your building, you see your director's parking space. In front of the space is a sign that says: "Reserved for Department Director." The parking space is empty. Reserved parking spaces are symbols which clearly demonstrate to lower-level employees that the organization views them as less valuable than those at the top of the hierarchy.

There are other subtle signs of a negative attitude towards subordinates. When employees learn news about their organization through a local newspaper or a source other than the organization itself, it displays a lack of respect for the employees. When managers make decisions that negate the careful and hard work of their employees, they demonstrate that they do not trust or respect their employees' work.

When an organization treats its employees with trust and respect, it demonstrates that it expects those same behaviors throughout the organization. It shows alignment between spoken goals and actions, reducing frustration, Non-Useful Work, and Heat. In the absence of a negative attitude towards

---

[1] Face Time with Meg Whitman, Fast Company, Issue 46, Page 72, May 2001,
http://www.fastcompany.com/magazine/46/facetime.html

subordinates, employees can be motivated to work passionately and creatively towards the organization's spoken goals without wasted energy due to Friction.

Example: **AirSPACE**

Negative Attitude Towards Subordinates

Blake
Sales

The sales division in AirSPACE has a compensation structure composed of salary and commission. Employees in sales have a relatively low salary but can be compensated quite well due to AirSPACE's commission structure.

Blake has been a salesman for AirSPACE for five years. He is an excellent performer and, last year, won the award for the most sales. He has seen business decline since he began and has been through two rounds of layoffs within the sales division. He had been very happy working in AirSPACE until last year, when the sales division began changing the commission structure.

The commission structure was the key to high compensation. Sales employees planned their days around their objectives as determined by the commission structure. They were paid according to a mix of how many calls they made, how many clients they maintained, and the total dollar amount of sales they generated. The commission structure was very effective in determining how everyone in Sales approached their jobs.

Last October, the division announced an unexpected change to the commission structure. They said they were better aligning the sales division to AirSPACE's business needs. It only had a minor impact on how Blake would be compensated, though it did reduce his take-home pay by 2% for the year. He was annoyed that he lost a little bit of money, but he was more frustrated that management would make a change to such a major policy which affected the take-home pay of many employees. Blake rearranged his workday in order to maximize his pay according to the new commission structure. He finished out the year successfully in spite of the change.

It was now September of the following year, and the commission structure had already been modified *three times*. Blake and his colleagues were frustrated; morale was lower than he had ever seen it. Each change to the structure was unexpected. Blake's supervisor kept telling him that the changes were for the benefit of both AirSPACE and the employees. In addition, after each change, the supervisor said it would be the last one for the year. Blake could not calculate whether he was gaining or losing commission because the structure grew more complex with each change. Further, Blake did not know whether business conditions were changing quickly or whether those setting the commission structure were unskilled at doing so.

These commission structure changes had many negative effects. Sales employees spent more time complaining about their jobs. People were more disengaged in meetings. They grew more suspicious of AirSPACE, wondering every day whether they would need to rearrange their approach to work *again*.

Rearranging the pay structure is an example of the negative attitude towards subordinates. Changing someone's pay structure is a major event. Changing it frequently and without advanced communication or adequate explanation is disrespectful. The lack of communication by the organization indicates that it does not view the change as an important event. This implies to the people affected by the change that the organization believes they are not important.

How should employees react to this? They see these changes as inappropriate, frustrating, and demeaning. After the initial change, it is appropriate for employees to voice their concerns regarding how they will be affected. However, repeated changes reflect the physics of the organization. AirSPACE is indicating that it does not view these changes as significant, since they altered the structure three times in nine months. If sales employees continued to push for an explanation or a promise not to make future changes, they would simply be creating Heat. AirSPACE would have already made these explanations or promises if they thought it was important. When an organization makes such significant changes to pay structures or job descriptions without fully informing employees, it makes a statement about how it values its workers. It also makes a clear statement that behaviors which discount the core needs of subordinates are acceptable.

A negative attitude towards subordinates indicates that the organization expects the following from its employees:
- Deference to position power
- Unconditional respect from subordinates
- No differing ideas and opinions

It also provides the ability to give and deflect blame to those lower in the organization. When you observe a negative attitude towards subordinates, your organization is communicating its acceptance of the above behaviors.

Ambient Sources: Probe Deeper to Understand What They *Really* Want

The existence of an Ambient Source of Friction means there are unspoken goals which you must understand and consider in order to avoid creating Heat. Sources of Friction, revealed by the behaviors you observe, indicate organization-wide attitudes which your organization expects you to accept. Sources of Friction show you how you must set your interface and work to get things done.

How do you know when you are in the presence of an Ambient Source of Friction?

> **Probe for Ambient Sources of Friction** when you feel frustrated that something does not make sense or is not "right." There are usually explainable reasons for frustrating and confusing situations. Probing deeper shows you what your organization *really* wants.

Point Sources of Friction

Ambient Sources of Friction exist on the organizational level, revealing behaviors and attitudes which are pervasive throughout the organization. Point Sources of Friction, however, exist on an individual level. A Point Source of Friction is someone whose goals and objectives are different than the stated goals of the organization. One example of a Point Source is someone who works to increase the size of his or her section or department despite a lack of benefit to the organization. Another example is someone who causes tension within the organization for no apparent reason. These examples are Point Sources of Friction because they want something different than what the organization *says* it wants.

Point Sources are motivated by a well-defined set of goals. It is easy, but not useful, to simply label someone as "difficult." Friction shows disconnects between what the organization *says* it wants and what people *really* want. It is at these disconnects where you must look deeper to understand someone's goals. When you encounter someone who causes you to think "This person is difficult" or "This person doesn't care," you are receiving a cue to Probe deeper to understand what that person *really* wants.

> **Probe for Point Sources of Friction** when your impulse is
> to call someone "lazy," "uncooperative," "stupid," or any
> other negative label. There is usually a well-defined set of
> goals driving a Point Source's behavior. Probing deeper
> shows you what that person *really* wants.

Point Sources actively get in the way of progress within the organization. They are ready to convert your Organizational Energy into Non-Useful Work or Heat. Regardless of their specific goals, Point Sources are dangerous because they do not have your or the organization's best interests in mind. They are more than willing to help you create Heat and shrink your box if you engage them. Worse, they may channel Heat in your direction if you get in their way.

Point sources of Friction are easy to identify by watching behavior and listening to colleagues. You can identify Point Sources in many ways:

- Point Sources' behaviors and actions do not support the stated goals of the organization.
- Point Sources behave differently in the presence of their superiors.
- Point Sources are frequently talked about negatively. While it is important to remain objective when listening to others' opinions of a person, a person who is constantly accused of negative political behavior may be a Point Source of Friction.
- Point Sources will ask you for information, then use that information subversively.
- Point Sources believe their knowledge makes them powerful. They will withhold critical information in order to use it for their benefit.
- Point Sources make underhanded, demeaning, and accusatory comments, especially when not in their superior's presence.

What do Point Sources of Friction *Really* Want?

Since every person is different, a Point Source may *really* want something different than another Point Source. The best way to determine what they *really* want is to observe their behavior. See when they act differently in the presence of others and determine why they do this. Watch them closely and listen to the questions they ask, as in the example below.

Example: *AirSPACE*
Point Source of Friction

Dave
Supervisor

|

Bryant
Engineer

Bryant identified a supervisor named Dave as a Point Source of Friction. Bryant's colleagues observed that those who did not get along with Dave seemed to be moved to other areas. As such, Dave developed a reputation for not tolerating differing opinions. What did Dave *really* want?

Everything Dave *really* wanted came out in a one-minute exchange with Bryant. One day, a Tool Shop supplier asked Bryant if he could bring his production manager to tour the facility and observe how their parts were being used. The supplier also said they were visiting one of AirSPACE's competitors the day before.

Bryant knew he needed permission from his management to set up this visit. Since there were no other supervisors to ask, Bryant needed to approach Dave. Before he did, he thought about how he would ask Dave for his permission to allow this visit. What was in it for Dave? Bryant decided he would offer this as an opportunity for Dave to learn about their competitor by getting information from the supplier. Bryant said to himself: "If Dave was interested in making improvements in his area, he would want to know what his competitor was doing." He checked Dave's schedule and verified that Dave was available at the time of the visit.

When Bryant approached Dave, the first question Dave asked was about the supplier's manager: "What is his full title?" Bryant told Dave that the visitor was a production manager, which Dave knew was a low-level position at the supplier. Then Bryant presented Dave the opportunity to get information from the supplier about their competitor's operations. Dave replied: "Oh, we visited their facility two years ago…I don't need to know anything more about them."

It is possible that there was nothing Dave could gain from a discussion with the production manager. However, after Dave learned that the visitor was a lower-level manager, he lost all interest in the supplier's visit.

From this exchange, Bryant determined that Dave was *really* interested in position power, as indicated by the very first question he asked. Dave did not appear to value discussions with people who did not have position power. Second, Bryant considered that Dave may not *really* be interested in improving his own operation, since he declined an opportunity to learn current information about his competitor. Bryant recognized that he could not make firm judgments about people and their motivations based on a single interaction. However, Dave's behavior in this encounter matched Dave's previous behaviors, so Bryant accepted this as more data to confirm what he already believed.

What does Dave's behavior in this situation suggest about how Bryant must act? Dave believes position power is very important. Bryant must be careful and respectful around Dave. Bryant must respect his attitude towards position power and, when required, must defer to Dave's position. Dave must be confident that Bryant knows his place within his organization. Bryant likes to share articles from manufacturing magazines with his colleagues on how to improve their jobs. He must not share these technical articles with Dave, who may view this as a challenge to his power, knowledge, and management skills.

Unfortunately, there are individuals in every organization whose goals are simply not aligned with the organization's goals. These people present opportunities for you to create Heat and shrink your box. You must Probe these Point Sources to learn what they *really* want. You must tune your interface so, when faced with a situation where you must work with them, you can avoid creating Heat and give them what they *really* want so they do not keep you from getting what you *really* want.

The Finer Points of Friction

Friction is an opportunity for you to learn what your organization *really* wants. However, if you interact inappropriately with Friction, it can be a source of pain and frustration. Rubbing against Friction and creating Heat will shrink your box and keep you from getting what you *really* want. You must understand that Friction persists because it benefits someone. In addition, you must recognize that you are unable to change the Friction in your organization.

Friction's continued existence is a sign that it serves a purpose for someone. Friction has been around longer than most of the organization's current members. Most people who are high in the organization know about the Friction. While working their way up to their position, they have experienced the frustrating and inefficient Sources of Friction that others currently struggle with. *Those high in the organization's hierarchy have the power to fix the Friction if they want to.* The fact that it remains is a clear statement that **someone with power has made a conscious decision to allow the Friction's**

existence. They *could* fix the Friction if they wanted to but they *do not* fix it because someone is, in some way, benefiting from it.

How could someone benefit from Friction? Friction enables people to channel the flow of power within an organization. Friction can be used to guide the flow of resources to areas that do not best suit the organization's interests. It can be used to establish territories which inhibit teamwork and reduce the flow of information. Finally, it can be used by people within the organization to help them defend themselves against unhealthy politics.

Those who are successful in a High-Friction Organization adjust to the presence of Friction and factor it into their daily approach to work. Situations are rational and understandable when you account for Friction's presence. If a bureaucracy is larger than it needs to be, something in the organization's resource allocation process has resulted in its excessive size. Because people respond effectively to how they are measured, rewarded, and promoted, those in the bureaucracy are behaving rationally in that context. In a High-Friction Organization, a bureaucracy manager does not have a vested interest in fixing the Friction caused by their oversized department. If they reduce their department's size, they may reduce their own power, influence, compensation and ability to direct resources. Even if they wanted to reduce the Friction, they may be limited if someone else is actively using the bureaucracy to forward their own agenda. Once Friction is established, it is very difficult to eliminate.

Because only certain people can fix Friction, it is especially dangerous to employees who earnestly wish to make improvements. Do-the-right-thing employees see a problem and they want to fix it; if something is not right, they want to make it right. Unfortunately, only those who are high in the organization's hierarchy can fix Friction. Friction benefits *someone* who is generally high in the organization's hierarchy and, therefore, is powerful. When people at lower levels try to fix Friction, they are threatening to change a structure which benefits that powerful person or group. Their efforts to fix Friction will be resisted and, more than likely, the person trying to make the change will be punished. It is for this reason that do-the-right-thing people become frustrated working in High-Friction Organizations: they see that something does not match the organization's stated goals and they cannot understand why they are being punished for trying to make it right.

Friction is damaging because it is invisible *and* it can hurt your efforts to make positive change. Friction is, by definition, hidden to people who do not know to look for it. As most employees are unaware of Friction, they regularly rub against it and create Heat. When the organization decides how it will distribute promotions, raises, and bonuses, it will reward those people who know how to give it what it *really* wants. It will not reward employees who create Heat, no matter how good their intentions. When you create Heat, your organization will not reward you but will, instead, give you a smaller box, smaller rewards, and less flexibility.

Recall the Law of Conservation of Organizational Energy. The unspoken goals which lead to Organizational Friction reduce the amount of Useful Work that can be accomplished. More people in the organization will create Heat, leading to frustration and aggravation for the organization's members. Finally, Friction causes the despair of the Low Level of Pain that employees feel when they believe that their organization is capable of more than the Friction within it will allow.

Why Friction Persists in Organizations

Friction develops when job specialization is not effectively managed. There are, however, other reasons that Organizational Friction develops and is reinforced. Those reasons are not widely discussed because they are distasteful. Friction, over time, enables some within the organization to wield power to direct and control resources. People who know how to take advantage of Friction can use it for great benefit. While specialization is one cause of Friction, people who are not aligned with the organization's stated goals can lead to the establishment and reinforcement of Friction.

As Point Sources of Friction gain power and influence or develop a comfortable territory at work, they continuously work to reinforce what they have gathered or built. They make key decisions, such as promotion decisions, performance evaluations, and job assignments based on who will best help them meet their own needs at the expense of the organization. The organization as a whole may still passionately pursue its goal to make great products and services. However, there will be areas in which employees will be driven to put a Point Source's needs for power, influence, or work arrangement above the organization's true goals. This will generate Non-Useful Work. Pockets will begin to develop where unspoken goals are different from the organization's spoken goals.

As Friction persists, fear becomes a mechanism which cements Friction into the organization. Fear is paralyzing and pervasive. Over time, people at all levels adapt to fear and learn to avoid pain, setting up defensive structures to keep themselves safe from harm. Employees are no longer entirely focused on the organization's best interests; rather, they are partially focused on self-preservation. When well-intentioned employees inadvertently try to improve something which impacts someone else's defensive structure, those well-intentioned employees will be punished by the person who has found a way to keep themselves safe.

In summary, fear leads to the establishment of defensive structures to help people stay safe in a dangerous environment. It is no longer just specialists and Point Sources who *really* want something different than what the organization *says* it wants. Almost everyone in the organization, partially driven by fear, acts in ways that are contrary to the organization's spoken goals. Friction transforms from a collection of Point Sources into Ambient Sources. Employees who are successful in such an organization have learned to work in a way that does not challenge the agendas of those who are driven for power, territory, safety, or a comfortable work arrangement. Successful employees work in ways that do not challenge the defensive structures that others have constructed to stay safe in the midst of fear. The organization's Friction-level has increased and Organizational Energy is now converted into larger amounts of Non-Useful Work and Heat and into a smaller amount of Useful Work.

The following example shows how the Ambient Source of Friction of a negative attitude towards subordinates causes fear in employees, negatively changing the way they work.

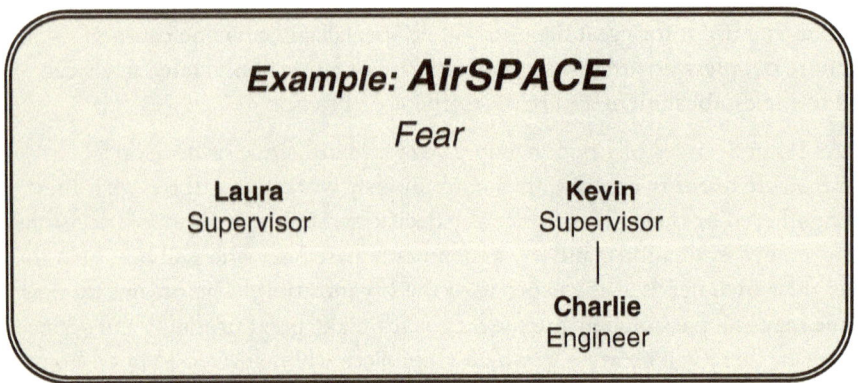

Charlie sat alone in his cubicle. He knew he had been floundering on his project. He had even joked with his colleagues that he could be fired any day. There was little likelihood this would happen, regardless of how badly his project went. However, he was a very capable and motivated employee who wanted to make great things happen and he felt very apprehensive about his inability to make progress on the project.

It was, indeed, a very difficult assignment. He was to lead an organizational improvement project and work with three high-level managers from different departments. He had not received much instruction regarding what he was to deliver or what was expected from him. He met with his management several times to share his ideas but, each time he met with them, he never seemed to deliver what they were looking for.

Charlie had just come from a meeting where he thought he would finally get some clear direction. He had been on the project for eight weeks and was just as confused as when he first started. He had received differing directions from each of the high-level managers in the past month. He had finally gotten them all into a single room to discuss the project's status and direction. He anticipated the opportunity to hear all three managers speak their positions and come to an agreement on what should be done.

Unfortunately, by the end of the meeting, Charlie could still not see a clear path for the project; he could not even figure out what to do next. He really wanted his project to succeed because he saw the huge benefits to AirSPACE of success. Not wanting to let this opportunity pass for getting clarity of the assignment, he said, just as the meeting was breaking up: "I still don't understand what direction we want to take on this project." One of the high-level managers who was outside of Charlie's immediate organization started to list some things the team should do. As everyone was leaving the room, Charlie heard his manager, Kevin, tell someone: "If you have any questions on this project, Brian will be your contact." Nobody had told Charlie that he was off the project but, apparently, the decision had been made. Charlie returned to his office and sat quietly. He felt horrible; he was shocked, confused, and uncertain. He felt powerless to make anything positive happen. These feelings began to coalesce into a fear of what might happen next.

Two hours later, Laura stopped by to see Charlie. Charlie had previously worked for Laura. Laura said: "Charlie, I hear things aren't going well on your project." Charlie answered: "Yeah, it's not good. It seems that I'm off the project, though nobody has told me anything." Laura sat down. She said: "Look, Charlie, you've upset a few people over the last few weeks. I don't know everything that's happened. But Kevin talked to me; he said he's getting together with the other managers in the area. They're going to put their heads together and develop a list of skills and behaviors you need to improve. You've got some really great talents and capabilities. I'd hate to see you pigeon-holed at this stage in your career."

After Laura got up and left, Charlie just stared out the window. He was floored. Kevin still hadn't officially told him he was off the project. Now his management was questioning his career potential and putting together a summary of his flaws! He felt like he was being punished, even though he had only tried to do his best for AirSPACE throughout the project. It was near quitting time, so Charlie went home.

He arrived the next morning with the same pit in his stomach that he left with the night before. It was Thursday and he had no idea what he would work on that day. He had not heard anything at all from Kevin on what was happening. Charlie passed the time in his cubicle for most of the day. Charlie wanted to see Kevin but he figured that, if Kevin wanted to tell him something, he would come to his cubicle. The day passed and Kevin never stopped by.

Friday was the same experience. He arrived at work feeling horrible and directionless. He was especially apprehensive because there was a company holiday on the upcoming Monday and Charlie was faced with a three-day weekend, which he would spend entirely in the dark about what was happening with his job. Would he be fired? Would he be demoted? What would he do when he arrived to work on Tuesday?

Charlie was moved to a new assignment later the following week. Kevin finally spoke with Charlie about the need to remove him from the project, since it clearly did not fit his skill set. The managers, as promised, put together a 1-page list of character traits that Charlie needed to improve. They were kind enough to include a "strengths" column alongside the "weaknesses," even though it appeared that the strengths they listed were minimal and forced.

Charlie left this assignment with an entirely different outlook at work. He was not quite as positive as before. He was less inclined to speak up in meetings, especially if he disagreed with his management. Most importantly, he distrusted his organization. Charlie had a first-hand experience with fear in AirSPACE, resulting in profound changes in how he approached his job. Charlie was previously unaware of Sources of Friction like negative attitudes towards subordinates. He had not understood that AirSPACE valued behavior over results. Before this experience, Charlie did not feel the fear that others within the organization occasionally spoke about. He had believed that as long as he tried to do a good job, he would not need to worry about something bad happening to him. By this experience, he had been clearly shown that he did not have enough respect for the culture within AirSPACE. His behavior was now tempered by fear. It was not fear that he would lose his job or be demoted; it was the fear that he would be treated harshly and would be made to feel inadequate and inferior.

Heat Creation is No Longer Just Painful

Even when you practice creating SPACE, you will invariably create Heat. Heat Creation means that you have interfaced inappropriately with a Source of Friction. When you create Heat, Friction reveals its presence as well as more information about what your organization *really* wants. Your Heat Creation experience now becomes an opportunity for learning.

If you create Heat, be sure to ask the following questions:

- How can I prevent the Heat I just created from causing me harm? (see the Execute chapter for an example of Heat mitigation)
- What was the Source of Friction that I rubbed against?
- Was the Source of Friction an Ambient Source or a Point Source?
- What does this tell me about what my larger organization *really* wants?
- What does this tell me about what individuals within my organization *really* want?
- How could I have avoided creating Heat?
- How can I avoid creating Heat in the future?

When you experience confusion or create Heat and you cannot detect a Source of Friction, make a mental note of the current circumstances to see if other confusing events unfold in a similar fashion. Recurring patterns indicate a Source of Friction that will reveal itself when you continue to observe the behaviors of those around you.

The ideal situation for using Heat to learn about your organization is to carefully observe situations when others create Heat. Everyone chooses whether or not they will create Heat. You can benefit from others who choose not to interface properly with your organization. Remember to watch Heat Creation situations and observe the resulting behaviors to learn what others *really* want.

When you or others create Heat, do not lose the opportunity to learn from the resulting pain. You can use what you learn to better tune your interface so you can increase the size of your box and get what you *really* want.

Probe - Conclusions

Behaviors are the keys to Probing deeply to understand what organizations and individuals within them *really* want. When you observe others' behaviors over time, you will learn what is truly important to them. When you understand what people *really* want, you can tune your interface to deliver your good work in the way people want it.

When you understand Friction, you will no longer be confused when you receive mixed messages from your organization. You will create less Heat and learn from the infrequent situations when you do create Heat. You will turn more of your Organizational Energy into Useful Work. Finally, you will be better equipped to deliver your great work in a way that your organization appreciates.

Example: *AirSPACE*

Tool Shop Utilization Report
Probe Implications

Andrew
Supervisor

|

Bryant
Engineer

Bryant was frustrated that he was being asked to put aside his one-page report showing how effectively the Tool Shop was being used. He was frustrated that Andrew, in front of Bryant's peers, asked him to put together a different report. He was weighing his options to decide whether he should push back on Andrew, risk creating Heat and getting a smaller box, or whether he should take some other action. In the midst of his frustration, Bryant stepped back and considered what Andrew *really* wanted.

Andrew has clearly demonstrated that he prefers to work without management scrutiny. Andrew has said he believes that management gets in the way of progress. Andrew also communicated that his single goal when senior management comes to tour the facility is to make them so happy that they will not want to come back again for two years. Bryant realized that what Andrew is asking him to do makes perfect sense when considering the request in the context of what Andrew *really* wants. Bryant has seen the implications of senior management's involvement in a project; they require endless presentations and reports on the project's status when they become involved. Bryant realized it was very possible that Andrew was going to work hard to fix the Tool Shop's problems. Andrew may just want to do it without the interference from senior management that would result in an inordinate amount of Non-Useful Work.

Bryant also recalled some other Ambient Sources of Friction within AirSPACE: a severe vertical hierarchy that requires endless reviews for approval and a negative attitude towards subordinates. Asking for a report that Bryant believed was non-useful could be Andrew's astute efforts to avoid Heat Creation.

Bryant believed he understood the Sources of Friction at work. He believed he knew what Andrew *really* wanted. Should he just deliver the report Andrew asked for? Bryant began to think about what he, himself, *really* wanted and how that impacted the current situation

---

Key Points from Probe:

1) Behaviors are the keys to understanding what organizations and people with them *really* want.

2) Friction shows itself at times when you perceive a disconnect between what the organization says it wants and behaviors that do not align with those spoken goals.

3) Friction can develop when specialists focus on their individual goals at the expense of the organization's goals.

4) Friction *always* benefits *someone*.

5) Ambient Sources of Friction show you how to tune your interface when you work outside of your natural work group.

6) Be wary around Point Sources of Friction.

7) If you try to fix Friction, you are challenging structures that have been consciously built to support power, territory, safety, or a work arrangement.

8) Friction is reinforced by fear.

9) You can use Heat Creation experiences as effective tools for learning about what your organization *really* wants.

Giving your organization what it *really* wants is only half of your employment agreement. Your organization has hired you to do a job, so it deserves your efforts and hard work. You have agreed to deliver your hard work and dedication. You must get your half of the agreement; you must get what you *really* want at work. Now that you have figured out what your organization *really* wants, focus on understanding what you *really* want.

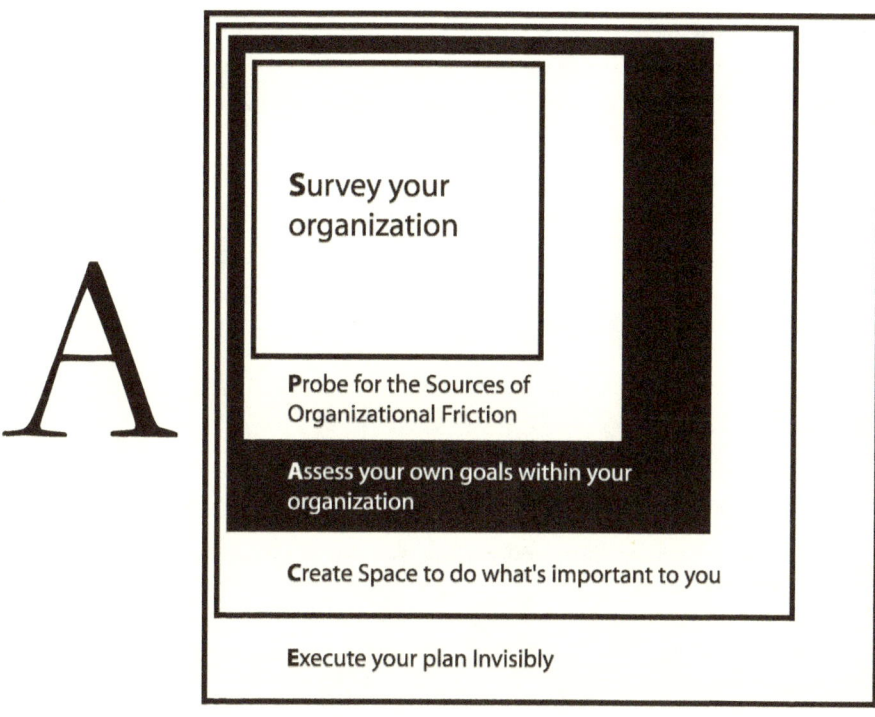

A

Survey your organization

Probe for the Sources of Organizational Friction

Assess your own goals within your organization

Create Space to do what's important to you

Execute your plan Invisibly

To get what you *really* want through creating SPACE, you must know what you *really* want. This is not always straightforward because many people expend considerable energy fighting for outcomes that are not really important to them or their organizations. What you believe your goals to be will drive the way you behave. When you work towards goals which you believe are important, you are more passionate, engaged, and effective. You are more inclined to fight for what you think you *really* want. If you work for something you do not *really* want, you will not be satisfied with the results you get. You will act in ways that your organization does not appreciate, leaving you with a smaller box.

Modifying your interface with your organization requires energy. If you work in a High-Friction Organization, the energy you expend can be significant. To be successful in adjusting your interface, you must get something rewarding from your efforts. If you do not, you can become frustrated that you work so hard without a tangible return.

Assess will show you how to understand what you *really* want and how your goals can impact your success. The Assess chapter will:

- Define Self-Righteousness: it is the core of all Heat in an organization and it will keep you from getting what you *really* want.

- Use the Goals-Righteousness Model to explain Self-Righteousness in terms of Organizational Mechanics.
- Explore Self-Righteousness so you can better recognize it and stop it before it causes you to shrink your box.
- Present Assess-Accept-Act, which will help you clarify what you *really* want.
- Understand why some goals can lead you to create Heat.

Assess is about understanding what is *truly* important to you. It is also about understanding what is *not* important to you so you can avoid expending your energy working for those goals.

Self-Righteousness – the Core of All Heat

Understanding Self-Righteousness is the core of the SPACE process.

> **Self-Righteous**: *adjective* – Convinced of one's own righteousness, especially in contrast with the actions and beliefs of others: narrow-mindedly moralistic.
>
> - Merriam-Webster Dictionary

Self-Righteousness is the ultimate stumbling block that prevents you from getting what you *really* want. In terms of Organizational Mechanics:

> **Self-Righteousness is the core of all Heat.**

Self-Righteousness does nothing but waste energy. It leads to emotional reactions, causing people to act in ways which keep them from getting what they *really* want. Self-Righteousness does not help people develop win-win solutions and become valued employees. Instead, Self-Righteousness leads to win-lose and lose-lose outcomes. People who act out of Self-Righteousness will not be seen as team players. They will find their efforts constantly resisted. These Heat Creators channel their Organizational Energy and the energy of those around them into Heat. To get what you *really* want, you must be fully aware of Self-Righteousness and its effects.

The Goals-Righteousness Model

The Goals-Righteousness Model explains the impact of Self-Righteousness in an organization. Specifically, it shows:

- The effects of Friction, which are manifested by your organization's unspoken goals.
- The tension caused by your organization's unspoken goals and your desire to meet its spoken goals.
- The negative impact of acting out of Self-Righteousness.

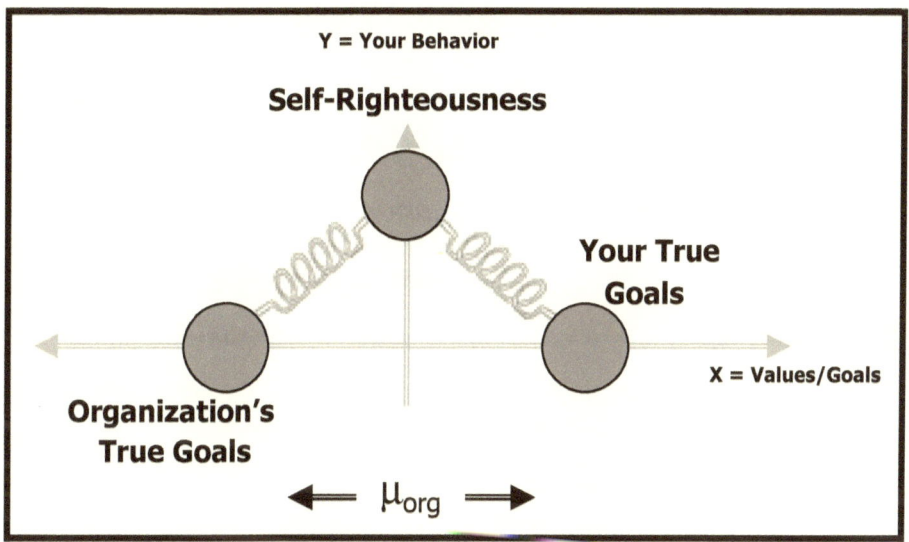

The Goals-Righteousness Model

The Goals-Righteousness Model begins by placing values and goals along an axis. One ball represents your true goals and values: what you *really* want and care about. Another ball represents your organization's true goals: what your organization *really* wants and cares about. The distance between those two balls is determined by the Friction in the organization.

> **Note:** In the Goals-Righteousness Model, you will see "μ_{org}." μ is the Greek symbol for the coefficient of friction. "μ_{org}" means "the friction level in the organization."

When you see your organization behave in ways which you perceive to be contrary to its stated goals, you sense the difference between your organization's true goals and stated goals. Have you ever heard an organization say: "We do not want to make a profit. Our company exists to perpetuate the status quo."? You would never actually hear this. However, everyone has seen their organization behave in ways that suggest it is not always interested in success. The Goals-Righteousness Model contains the underlying assumption that your true goals are the same as your organization's *spoken* goals. Most people join an organization expecting to support its spoken objectives. So, if the organization *says* it wants to make money, the Goals-Righteousness Model assumes you want to help it make money. Similarly, if the organization *says* it wants employees who are committed to positive change, the Goals-Righteousness Model assumes you will embrace change for your organization's benefit.

Example: *AirSPACE*

Goals-Righteousness Model

Issues Management Database

AirSPACE has design problems like any other company. When an employee finds a problem requiring a change to a product, they must enter that problem into a database called the "Issues Management Storage Utility for Product Development." The official acronym for this database is "the IMD" (the "Issues Management Database"). The database alerts management, helping them properly direct resources to quickly resolve problems. Too often in AirSPACE, however, the ultimate result of entering a problem into the IMD is punishment by management. As a result, most employees do not use this database. The IMD will be used throughout the discussion of the Goals-Righteousness Model to illustrate the Model's concepts.

The Goals-Righteousness Model – A No-Friction Organization

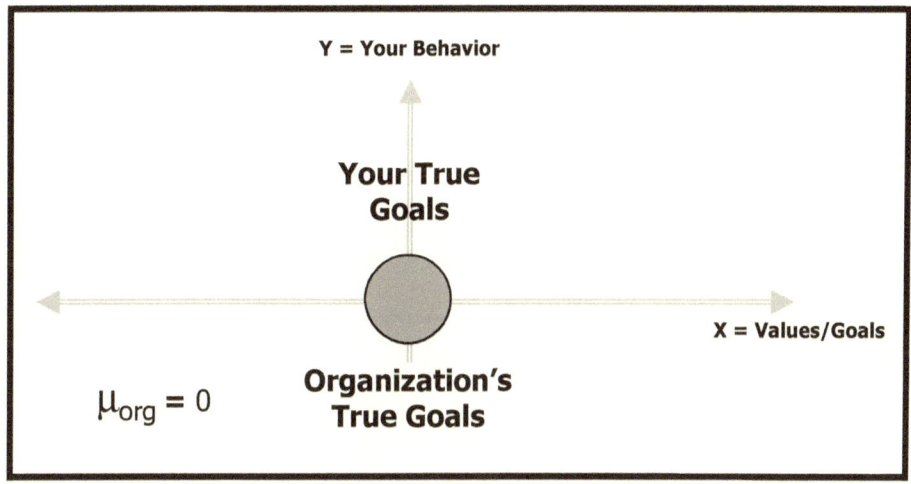

A No-Friction Organization

What is a No-Friction Organization? It is an organization that *really* wants what it says it wants. If the organization's mission statement says it values change agents, then change agents are truly valued and rewarded. If the organization's mission statement says it values customer service, employees are rewarded by providing superior customer service. There are very little politics in such an organization. What you hear and observe is a clear picture of reality and there are very few hidden agendas.

The Goals-Righteousness Model shows this situation with two overlapping balls which represent your true goals and your organization's true goals. In a No-Friction Organization, these two sets of goals are identical. The organization wants to make money and you want to help it make money. It values customer service and you practice exceptional customer service. There is no tension between you and your organization because you are both aligned with your goals. If your manager tells you to do something, you can take it at face value because everyone within the organization is aligned and working towards well-communicated and consistent goals.

What would Organizational Mechanics say about a No-Friction Organization? Most Organizational Energy would be converted to Useful Work. There would be very little Non-Useful Work, so employees would feel their energies were spent in worthwhile pursuits. There would be very little Heat, so employees would feel little pain from political missteps.

If AirSPACE was a No-Friction Organization, employees would be diligent about using the IMD without fear of punishment. Management would review items in the database and earnestly offer encouragement and support to the problem-solving teams. Teams who entered issues in the IMD would not be afraid of management reviews, since they are opportunities for help and support instead of opportunities for punishment.

Most people are not fortunate enough to work in a No-Friction Organization. Such an organization may not even exist. Moving closer to reality, consider an organization with a small amount of Friction.

The Goals-Righteousness Model – A Low-Friction Organization

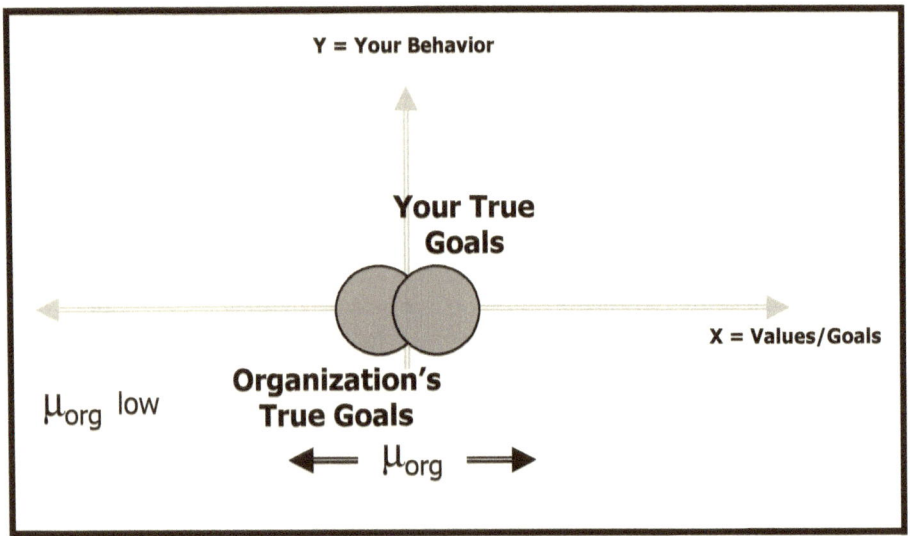

A Low-Friction Organization

The presence of Friction means that some within the organization really want something different than what the organization says it wants. As Friction develops, the organization begins to value things other than its publicized goals. Friction increases the distance between your true goals and your organization's true goals, causing the two balls above to spread apart. The Goals-Righteousness Model shows that, in a Low-Friction Organization, there is still significant overlap between your and your organization's true goals. You will not feel much tension because you are largely aligned with organizational goals. Accordingly, you will not need to Probe deeply into situations at work. While a Low-Friction Organization is not as efficient as a No-Friction Organization, most Organizational Energy will be converted into Useful Work. Working in a Low-Friction Organization can be rewarding, since what you really want and what your organization really wants are similar. However, notice what happens in the model as Friction continues to increase: the balls begin to move farther apart.

The Goals-Righteousness Model – Friction Increases Within the Organization

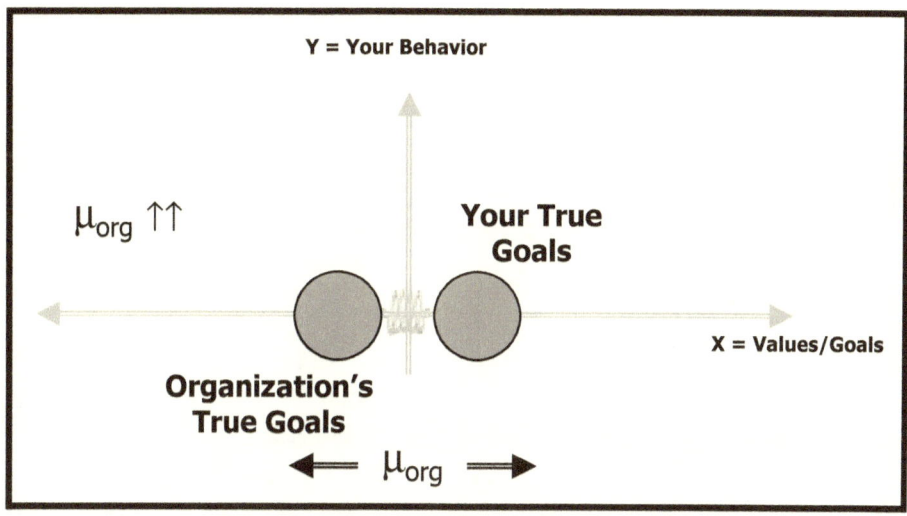

Increasing Friction within the Organization

As Friction continues to increase, your true goals and your organization's true goals move farther apart. When the distance becomes large enough, you will become aware of tension between you and your organization. Events at work will begin to confuse you in subtle ways. For example, your organization may say it wants you to be efficient but it will not always reward efficiency. Confusing experiences will not occur often, but you will feel a low level of frustration because the behaviors you observe will not always match what you are told. These situations cause tension, shown by a spring connecting your true goals and your organization's true goals. That spring represents the constant and unpleasant tug between you and your organization, always pulling on you to rub against Friction and create Heat.

How would employees in a Lower-Friction Organization feel about using the IMD? They would use it because it is not the blatant punishment tool that it is in AirSPACE. In a Lower-Friction Organization, management may occasionally punish people who are responsible for problems entered into the database. Yet, the IMD is generally used to help employees quickly resolve problems. Employees may not enter *all* relevant information about an issue into the database. There may be aspects of the problem that engineers do not want others to know for fear of reprisal. Ultimately, however, employees often use the IMD to report problems and management generally uses the system to provide support.

The Goals-Righteousness Model – A High-Friction Organization

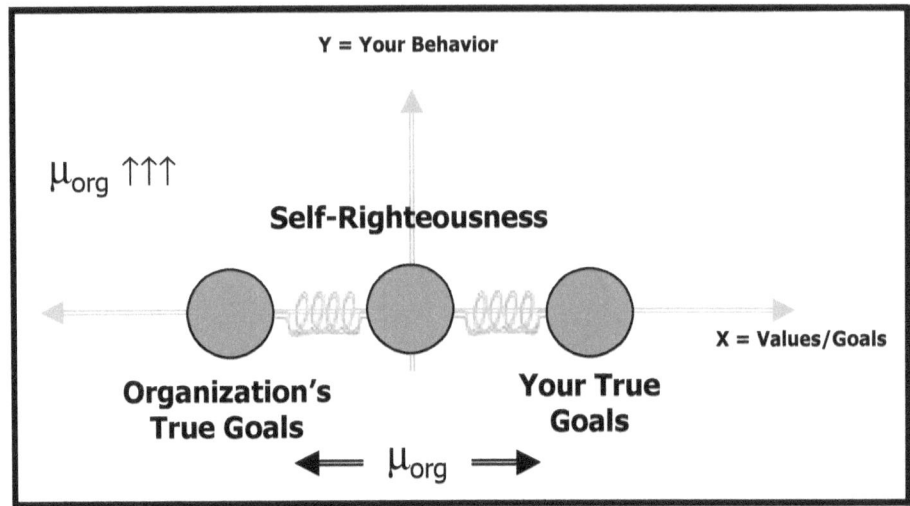

A High-Friction Organization

In a High-Friction Organization, there is considerable distance between your true goals and your organization's true goals. People act inconsistently with the organization's mission statement and published list of preferred behaviors. Employees operate from political agendas and there is more fear within the organization. People work to protect their own interests instead of the organization's interests. You may work for a supervisor who asks you to do things that do not seem to be aligned with what you believe your organization is striving for. Employees hide information from management and sometimes lie about data or the existence of problems.

The amount of Friction in the organization determines the distance between the balls representing your and your organization's true goals. That distance causes the spring to pull harder on you. That distance is the base level of tension – the Low Level of Pain – that you feel. Because you cannot change the Friction in your organization, you cannot change the distance between the balls or the base level of tension. As Friction increases, the tension between you and your organization increases. You will be frustrated because situations will be confusing and not make sense. You will begin to think things like: "I was trying to do the right thing; why did I just get punished for working for my organization's goals?" You may say: "This isn't right" or "This isn't fair." Self-Righteousness enters your thoughts and actions. As your frustration continues to increase, you will feel uncomfortable by confusing situations. If these events strike you as unfair or contrary to your view of your organization's goals, you will label the odd events that occur as 'wrong.' You will begin to think you are 'right' regarding what your organization's goals *should* be. You will begin to act out of Self-Righteousness against the things your organization *really* wants.

In the Goals-Righteousness Model, acting out of Self-Righteousness is shown by the Self-Righteousness ball moving up the *Your Behavior* axis. What does 'acting out of Self-Righteousness' mean? Consider a situation where you developed a presentation of your project for senior management. You have focused on a particular aspect of the project in the presentation, but your supervisor wants to focus on a different area. You believe your version demonstrates your project's key points more effectively, but your supervisor believes that senior management will ask unnecessary questions if your version is presented. You make your objections clear to your supervisor. Then, prior to delivering the presentation, you again voice your disagreement about its focus. At this point, voicing your objections is simply acting out of Self-Righteousness. You are convinced you are 'right' and know better than your supervisor how to present the project. It is possible you really do know better. However, to continue to push your point when you have been given clear direction is acting out of Self-Righteousness. Continuing to voice your concerns is represented by your Self-Righteousness ball moving upwards.

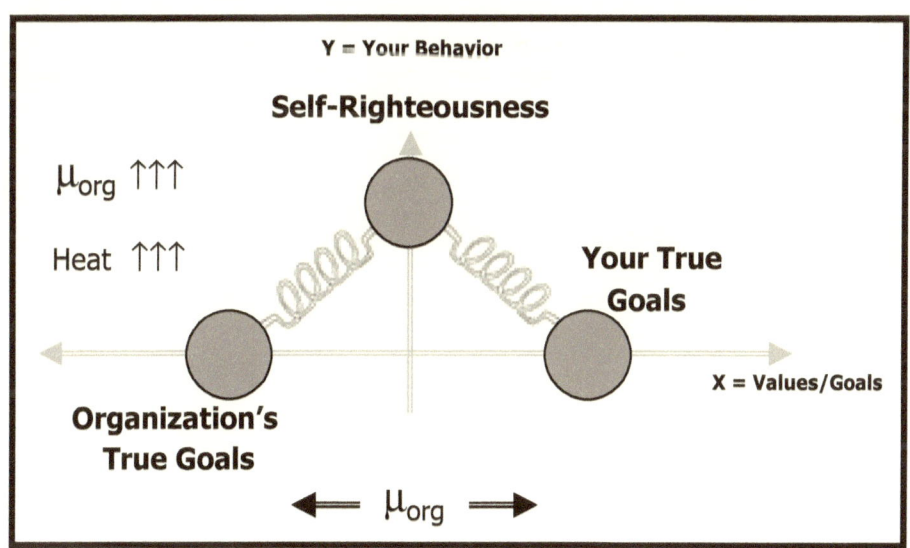

Acting out of Self-Righteousness in a High-Friction Organization

What are the effects of acting out of Self-Righteousness? The Goals-Righteousness Model shows that, as your ball moves higher on the *Your Behavior* axis, the tension within the organization increases. As you continue to act out of Self-Righteousness, the springs pull tighter and your actions further increase the tension. Increasing the tension in the organization creates Heat. When you create Heat, less Useful Work is accomplished according to the Law of Conservation of Organizational Energy. Creating Heat will keep you from getting what you *really* want.

> ## Friction is the Organization's problem –
> ## Heat is YOUR problem

Probe shows that you cannot fix the Friction in your organization. Friction benefits someone who is in a powerful position. It is a problem for your organization and can only be solved by someone higher than you. However, just because there is Friction does not mean there is Heat. Heat is created only when people act out of Self-Righteousness. Heat is created only when people cause unnecessary tension because they are convinced they are right and others are wrong. You are in full control as to whether you create Heat. Heat is *your* problem.

> ## You cannot control your organization's Friction level. You
> ## <u>can</u> control your Self-Righteousness.

According to the Goals-Righteousness Model, what is the best way to behave within your organization? See the diagram below:

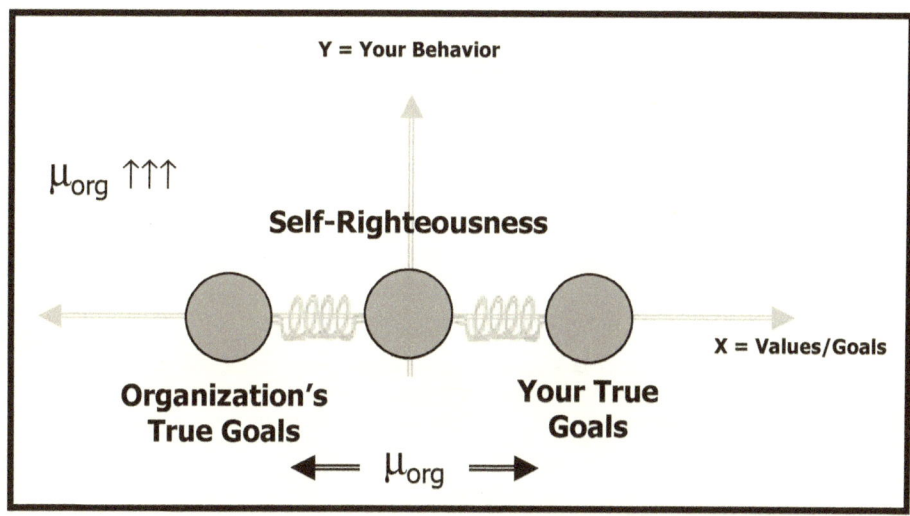

The Optimal Operating Location – CENTER YOUR BALL!

While you cannot control the distance between your and your organization's true goals, you *can* control how you behave within your organization. You control your Self-Righteousness. When you keep your Self-Righteousness ball centered, you work at the point of minimum tension with your organization. You will lose no energy due to Heat. If you keep your ball anywhere but centered, you will create Heat, which will shrink your box and keep you from getting what you *really* want. The diagram above shows the ideal operating location within a High-Friction Organization.

> **The optimal operating location in a High-Friction Organization is with your Self-Righteousness ball centered.**

The Goals-Righteousness Model shows why Centering Your Ball causes you to feel a Low Level of Pain. You feel the Low Level of Pain when you use your energy to contain your Self-Righteousness. In High-Friction Organizations, events constantly frustrate you; as a result, your Self-Righteousness ball's natural tendency is to move upwards. You must work hard and expend significant energy to pull your ball back to the center in the midst of Friction. This energy expenditure reduces the amount of Organizational Energy available for Useful Work and is shown as *Invisibility Pain* in the Law of Conservation of Organizational Energy.

Even with a centered ball, there is tension between you and your organization. The tension is present because you want something different than what your organization *really* wants. You *know* your organization can be more efficient. You *know* it can be more effective. However, you also understand the Law of Conservation of Organizational Energy, which illustrates how Friction reduces Useful Work. You know your organization will not always make choices that you define to be 'right.' This awareness causes constant frustration: the Low Level of Pain. The Low Level of Pain is the tension you feel, represented by the springs in the Goals-Righteousness Model.

The optimal operating location for anyone in a High-Friction Organization is to maintain composure and contain your Self-Righteousness. Keep your ball centered and you will work without creating Heat.

CENTER YOUR BALL!

Self-Righteousness Explored

Merriam-Webster defines Self-Righteousness to be:

Self-Righteous – *adjective* – Convinced of one's own righteousness especially in contrast with the actions and beliefs of others: narrow-mindedly moralistic.

– Merriam-Webster Dictionary

This definition shows how Self-Righteousness does not lead to win-win solutions; rather, it produces win-lose outcomes. Self-Righteousness is about your beliefs *in contrast* with the actions and beliefs of others. Viewing situations as 'right versus wrong' becomes a problem when you interface with others, because what is right and wrong for you may not be the same right and wrong for others. When you act out of Self-Righteousness, you act on your own sense of 'right' against someone else's sense of 'right.' You win. They lose.

Self-Righteousness moves beyond your thoughts to influence your actions. When you behave in ways that communicate to others that you believe you are right and they are wrong, those behaviors will not be valued by your organization. Colleagues and superiors will not view you as someone they want to help and support. The above definition calls Self-Righteousness "narrow-minded." Does "narrow-minded" describe the type of person you want to work with? Nobody wants a narrow-minded boss or colleague. Furthermore, nobody wants to promote someone they believe is narrow-minded. Narrow-minded people will be the last to receive rewards from the organization, not the first. Remember: when you act out of Self-Righteousness, you act in a way which is defined to be "narrow-minded."

Because SPACE is a behavior-based approach, it provides a behavior-based definition of Self-Righteousness:

Self-Righteousness - The confusion of your morals with your preferences and the behaviors and actions resulting from that confusion.

- SPACE Definition

You cause problems when you negate other people's preferences in favor of your own when there is no undisputable basis for doing so. There may be many different approaches to a situation. Everyone is entitled to their opinion regarding the best approach for meeting the organization's goals. Everyone has their own preference, just as you have your own preference. When you act out of Self-Righteousness, you create animosity and enemies. The simple daily acts of Self-Righteousness make you a liability to your organization. Acting out of Self-Righteousness creates Heat, shrinks your box, and keeps you from getting what you *really* want.

The Path to Controlling your Self-Righteousness

You must thoroughly understand Self-Righteousness so you can master it in all situations and keep your ball centered. To control your Self-Righteousness, you must first learn to recognize its presence. If you work in a High-Friction Organization, you likely have a large bank of experience of what Self-Righteousness feels like. Once you recognize the presence of Self-Righteousness, you can take steps to channel it in a way that does not create Heat. You can be sure your Self-Righteousness stays contained so it does not cause you to create Heat and get a smaller box.

Recognizing Self-Righteousness

One way to remember a situation when you acted out of Self-Righteousness is to remember a situation when you created Heat.

Example: *AirSPACE*

Self-Righteousness

Elizabeth
Engineer

Elizabeth was a young and motivated engineer at AirSPACE. Her current project was to work on jet engines for the South American market. Those customers began to experience engine problems, and frequently called AirSPACE engineers to get help to repair the engines. Elizabeth was fluent in Spanish, so she agreed to a temporary move to the customer relations department. She would take phone calls from South American technicians and would answer questions on how to fix the engines.

An assignment to customer relations was unusual for an engineer. Elizabeth would rather apply her engineering skills by designing engines. However, she recognized AirSPACE's need to help their customers and was happy to assist. She was promised that this assignment would last only three months.

Six months later, Elizabeth was still in customer relations and was frustrated. Management continued to assure her they were arranging her move back to engineering. Unfortunately, the move was continually pushed farther and farther into the future. In her latest meeting with management, Elizabeth was again told it would be at least another month before she could move back to engineering.

Elizabeth was frustrated. What was the delay?! She knew that every additional month spent in customer relations was a set-back for her career. She was an excellent performer. Furthermore, the entire reason she came to customer relations was to do AirSPACE a favor! She felt unappreciated and unrewarded for her loyalty. She complained to the engineering manager and demanded a written commitment for when she would be sent back to engineering.

Elizabeth's behavior was not well received by the engineering manager. She did not receive the written commitment she wanted. Worse, the engineering manager called Elizabeth's current manager to report her poor behavior. For the next three months, Elizabeth continued to feel the negative effects from her exchange with the engineering manager. She felt the effects of having a smaller box.

Elizabeth felt very Self-Righteous. She believed she went above and beyond the expectations for an AirSPACE employee and was not rewarded for it. As a result, she acted out of Self-Righteousness and created Heat. She earned a smaller box from this experience instead of the larger box she could have gotten from being a team player.

Consider a time when something happened to you and you knew it was not right. Recall a situation when you were not rewarded for something which you believed you *should* have been rewarded for. Did you push back against the Friction and create Heat? *It is through these experiences that you can readily recognize your Self-Righteousness!*

Situations where you feel Self-Righteousness have common characteristics:

- You make value-based statements in your head:
    o "This isn't right!"
    o "This isn't fair!"
    o "This is not a good use of our resources!"
    o "This is wasteful!"
    o "This is misleading!"
    o "Don't we have better things to do?!"

- You are confused when observed behaviors are inconsistent with spoken goals:
    o "This doesn't make any sense!"
    o "Why did *that* happen?!"
    o "Why didn't *that* happen?!"

- You are not rewarded for what you believe you should be rewarded for:
    o "Why doesn't someone recognize what I did?"
    o "Can't they see I was just trying to do the right thing?"

Reflect on your past experiences. Recall situations when you felt Self-Righteous. Remember the emotions: the confusion, the frustration and, perhaps, the anger. Become familiar with how these emotions feel so you can recognize them when you experience them again. During these times, you must recognize that your Self-Righteousness ball is elevated. SPACE provides tools to help you learn how to Center Your Ball. The first step to controlling your Self-Righteousness is to recognize its presence at the moment it occurs.

Turn Heat Creation into a Learning Experience

Have you been a Heat Creator? Changing your patterns of behavior that lead to Heat Creation is difficult and only happens over time. Along the way, you will experience situations where you create Heat. Now you can get more than just pain from those situations because you will be able to recognize them as encounters where you do not get what you *really* want and your box gets smaller.

Just as you used Heat Creation in Probe to understand Sources of Friction, you can use Heat Creation in Assess to better understand your Self-Righteousness. When you create Heat, you can immediately reflect on the emotions you were feeling as you were acting out of Self-Righteousness. You can become familiar with these emotions so you can recognize them earlier. You will learn more about your 'hot buttons' so you will be more aware of the types of situations that trigger your Self-Righteousness. You will, over time, become adept at avoiding Self-Righteous behavior.

A Final Note on Self-Righteousness – Why Crazy Promotions Happen

Do you ever wonder why certain people are promoted? Do you wonder why your organization rewards someone who you believe does not do the right thing? People who look out for their own interests do not get caught up in Self-Righteousness when they are asked to do something. They do not spend time and emotional energy considering whether an action will benefit the organization. They are less concerned about what is right or wrong for their organization than they are about what is right or wrong for themselves. They give the organization what it *really* wants so they can get what they *really* want. This enables them to let crazy things happening around them simply roll off their backs. They do not become frustrated by anything in their organization except what keeps them from getting what they *really* want. Organizations appreciate people who do not create Heat and will reward them accordingly.

Assess – Accept – Act

What do you *really* want?

Self-Righteousness will keep you from getting whatever it is you *really* want. When you learn to control your Self-Righteousness, what is the prize that you will receive? What will you receive for the hard work of keeping your ball centered?

Figuring out what you *really* want is not as easy as it sounds. Hardly anyone is asking you what *you* really want. When was the last time your supervisor asked you what you want out of life? When was the last time someone tried to understand what is important to you? If someone asked you what is *truly* important to you, could you answer that person without hesitation? After determining what you *really* want, what would you do if you realized that you simply could not get that from your organization?

To help you to get what you *really* want at work, SPACE provides the three-step Assess tool: Assess – Accept – Act. This tool will help you understand what you *really* want by considering your goals through the perspective of SPACE. Your goals may have Friction and Heat implications; certain goals will make you susceptible to acting out of Self-Righteousness and creating Heat. Assess – Accept – Act also views your goals across multiple time horizons to help you put your *Really* Wants into perspective.

> **Really Wants** – Goals you determine to be what you *really* want after they are filtered through Assess – Accept – Act.

SPACEable Goals

Certain goals can greatly affect your behavior and make you prone to creating Heat. Some goals are *SPACEable* and some are not.

> **SPACEable Goal** – A goal which will not cause you to create Heat in the course of trying to reach your goal.

Likewise, a non-SPACEable goal is one that will drive you to create Heat.

You must ensure that your goals are SPACEable so you can increase the size of your box and get what you *really* want. If you choose a non-SPACEable goal, you will create Heat while trying to achieve your goal. Therefore, before you determine what you *really* want, you must understand how to distinguish between SPACEable and non-SPACEable goals.

A SPACEable goal meets three criteria:

1) It is attainable.
2) It is elemental.
3) It does not contain Self-Righteousness.

Attainable Goals

An attainable goal is one you can achieve within your organization. Nothing is more frustrating than wanting something you will never get. When you set a goal which is not attainable within your organization, you will become frustrated that you have not achieved your goal. Your frustration will lead you to create Heat, leaving you with a smaller box.

Understanding attainability is not straightforward because of the mixed messages High-Friction Organizations send. It is easy to become confused and expect that some things are attainable when they really are not. Attainability is defined *by your organization*; it is not what *you* believe you should be able to achieve. To understand what your organization defines to be attainable, use what you learned in Probe: observe behaviors. Your organization's actions will, over time, indicate what goals it deems to be attainable.

Example: AirSPACE

Attainable Goals

Blake
Sales

Blake is the AirSPACE salesman who was the subject of the Probe example demonstrating Ambient Friction. Blake was frustrated that he did not have a stable commission structure around which he could plan his daily efforts. It seems reasonable to expect that the rules by which he earns his pay should be firm and unchanging. However, if that was the goal Blake *really* wanted, he was setting himself up for frustration. AirSPACE management has clearly demonstrated that they are not concerned about keeping the commission structure stable. Their actions indicate that this is not important to them. Blake's frustration with the changing commission structure is as useful as frustration with the laws of physics. Blake must realize that his goal of a stable commission structure is non-SPACEable because, based on observed behaviors, it is not attainable. He must adjust his expectations of how AirSPACE management will provide commission structures or recognize that this expectation will set him up to feel frustration and create Heat.

Elemental Goals

An elemental goal is one that cannot be broken down into smaller components. 'Getting paid to do a good job' is actually a combination of two individual goals: 'Getting paid' and 'doing a good job.' An elemental goal is the core of what you *really* want, as shown in the following example:

> ### *Example: Middle School*
> ### *Elemental Goals*
>
> #### Ellen
> Librarian

A middle school librarian used the concept of elemental goals to help her to clarify what she *really* wanted, resulting in major changes in how she felt about work and how she was viewed by her organization. Ellen was frustrated because she wanted a teaching position in her school district. She had just earned her Master's degree and was ready to get the position of "teacher." After two years as a librarian, she was frustrated that teaching positions within the school district were not available. Her management began to tell her that teaching positions would not be available for a long time. Her frustration caused her to act in ways that rubbed her colleagues and superiors the wrong way.

Then Ellen thought about what she *really* wanted. She thought that she really wanted to work closely with kids. As a librarian, she worked with kids throughout the day. As she thought more about the teacher position, she realized that, as a teacher, she would work closely with kids, but would have the added stress of preparing lesson plans, grading papers, satisfying requirements, and other responsibilities she really did *not* want. When she reduced her goal to an elemental goal, she realized that she was *already* getting what she *really* wanted. As a result, she was better able to focus on the kids who came through the library, develop new and innovative programs, and be satisfied that she had a job where she received many benefits without incurring the additional requirements which would have taken her away from her students.

When Ellen recognized her elemental goal, the changes to her life at work were striking. Her attitude greatly improved. She became adept at giving her organization what it *really* wanted. It began to reward her for her new interface. She began to get things she asked for on a regular basis. Reflecting on the changes, she said: "I started getting everything I asked for – I ran out of things to ask for!"

If your goals are elemental, you will not work towards a goal you do not *really* want. You will be less frustrated and better equipped to contain your Self-Righteousness in potential Heat Creation situations.

Goals which are Free of Self-Righteousness

The third component of a SPACEable goal is that it must not contain Self-Righteousness. A goal which contains Self-Righteousness will cause you to create Heat. Goals contain Self-Righteousness when they can be interpreted differently by different people. Self-Righteous goals cause you to think that you are right and others are wrong. They are easily identified by judgmental words, such as 'good' or 'fair.' If your goal is to 'do a good job,' other people can define a 'good job' differently than you do. This will cause disagreements regarding whether the goal was adequately achieved. Objective goals will ensure that everyone understands the same vision of 'success,' eliminating the possibility of conflict.

Therefore, to ensure that your goals are free of Self-Righteousness, different people must be able to view your goal in the same way you do. One way to test for Self-Righteousness is to ask the following question:

> ## Would a Point Source of Friction see your *Really* Want the same way you do?

If the answer is 'yes,' your goal is free of Self-Righteousness. If the answer is 'no,' your goal is not free of Self-Righteousness and it is non-SPACEable. You will be unable to achieve a non-SPACEable goal in a High-Friction Organization.

Remember that a Point Source of Friction is someone whose goals are different from your and your organization's goals. Words like 'good' and 'right' mean something different to Point Sources. For that reason, a Point Source's perspective provides a good reference for whether or not your goals contain Self-Righteousness.

Compare a list of SPACEable and non-SPACEable *Really* Wants:

SPACEable Goals	Non-SPACEable Goals
Money	Do a good job
Power	Fair pay
Promotion	Equity
Leave work at a certain time	Reward/ Recognition
Don't work weekends	The "right" thing

SPACEable Goals are SPACEable because they are attainable, elemental, and free of Self-Righteousness. For example, a certain level of income is attainable if you have the proper skills required by your organization. Money is certainly elemental. Money is free of Self-Righteousness. A Point Source sees money the same way that you do. If you say that you want to make $100,000 per year, it means exactly the same thing to a Point Source. Power, the ability to allocate resources and direct work, is attainable, elemental, and free of Self-Righteousness. If you talk with a Point Source, they will likely see power in a similar way that you do.

Look at some of the non-SPACEable goals to understand what makes them non-SPACEable. Would a Point Source believe that 'doing a good job' means the same thing to them as it does to you? They would not, since 'good' is a relative word and means something very different to people with dissimilar goals. 'Reward' or 'recognition' have different meanings for different people. Some consider recognition to be a monetary award, whereas others consider a simple "thank you" to be adequate recognition. A key to identifying non-SPACEable goals is to look for words that engender Self-Righteousness: good, fair, equitable, valuable, and right.

You cannot achieve a non-SPACEable goal in a High-Friction Organization. When you have goals that are filled with Self-Righteousness, you require your organization to value things the same way you value them. When you accomplish something you believe is 'good,' you want others to recognize your 'good' efforts. This sets up expectations that are frequently unmet. As a result, your Self-Righteousness ball rises and you are prone to creating Heat. These unrealistic expectations cause *so* much frustration for people, resulting in smaller boxes.

Note that SPACEability can change over time. Goals which are free from Self-Righteousness at one point in time may generate Self-Righteousness at another. Consider the goal of a promotion. This is attainable if you know how to deliver to your organization what it *really* wants and if economic conditions are such that your organization is promoting its employees. A promotion is elemental; it is not a mix of two or more goals. Is a promotion free from Self-Righteousness? It depends on how you feel about the promotion. If your attitude is: "I am going to work in a way to get this promotion and I'm not going to be frustrated that I don't have it," then this is free of Self-Righteousness. If, however, you see someone receive a promotion who you believe is unworthy, you may think: "Why did *that* person get promoted – is my organization crazy? *I* should have been promoted!" You may feel the tension between your organization's spoken and unspoken goals. Your Self-Righteousness ball may start to rise. You may suddenly become discontent that you have not been promoted. The promotion has now changed from a

SPACEable goal to a non-SPACEable goal. If you do not adjust your expectations accordingly, that non-SPACEable goal will cause you to act out of frustration and create Heat.

In Assessing what you *really* want, aim for goals that are SPACEable. Aim for goals that are attainable and specific. Aim for goals that are free from Self-Righteousness so you do not become frustrated and create Heat during the process of trying to reach those goals. When you determine your SPACEable *Really* Wants, you set yourself up for success within your organization. More importantly, you will find you are far less frustrated than you were before. You will better contain your Self-Righteousness and give your organization what it *really* wants so you can get what you *really* want.

Assess-Accept-Act Continued

How important are your *Really* Wants? The things you *really* want are *at least* as important as what your organization wants from you.

Many people today work hard at their jobs, putting in long hours away from their families without due consideration for what they *really* want. They are accustomed to putting their own important needs aside for the needs of a large organization. They do not hold their own needs to be as important as their organization's. Why do so many people work long hours on a regular basis?

How important is what *you* really want...to you?

Work is a Two-Way Agreement

When you get a job, you enter into a two-way agreement. An organization agrees to hire you to perform a function. You agree to work in that organization because it will meet some of your needs. However, many people look for more than this from their organization; they seek fulfillment, meaning, and the opportunity to demonstrate usefulness and skill. However, no employment contract commits an organization to help an employee find self-actualization. Therefore, from the start, the agreement between you and your organization may feel one-sided.

You must be clear about what you *really* want because your organization will not provide more than pay, benefits, or anything beyond what is specified in your employment contract. Consequently, you must be the agent in charge of ensuring that you get what you *really* want. If you do not, nobody will. You deserve to get what you *really* want at work. Consider what you do for your organization. You spend 8-12 hours each day at your job. You spend time getting ready in the morning, then undertake a commute which can last as much as an hour. If you live in a place where there is snow in the winter, you have probably driven to work under hazardous conditions. Do you ever consider the fact that you sometimes risk your life and your health to come to work? You give an enormous amount to your organization. You are fully entitled to get something back. It is up to you to ensure that what you receive for your efforts is something you *really* want.

Knowing your *Really* Wants Helps you Accept Organizational Mechanics

The realities of Organizational Mechanics can be hard to accept. It is easier to accept the physics of your situation at work when you realize that you are getting what you *really* want. Much of what happens at work is out of your control and many of those things can frustrate you. When you can step back and realize you are still getting what you *really* want in spite of crazy things that happen, you will feel your stress and frustration disappear. You will realize that you do not need to be frustrated when you are getting what you *really* want.

These concepts apply to any organization, not only for the place where you work. Any time you make an explicit or implied agreement to be a part of an organization, you agree to give something with the expectation that you will receive something in return. You must be aware of what you *really* want from your affiliation with an organization since *you* are ultimately responsible for ensuring that you get what you *really* want.

Time Horizons

Not all *Really* Wants are created equal. You could list many things that are important to you. Depending on your values system, some items on your list will be more important than others. Their priority may be set because they are family-related, church-related, or work-related. Some items on your list may take priority because of the amount of effort required to achieve them. Some items on your list may take priority because of the time required to achieve them. As such, *Time Horizons* are useful for prioritizing those goals.

The Time Horizon is the point in the future at which you expect to achieve your goal. Saving for your kids' college may be important. That is a long-term goal; it is a goal with a long Time Horizon. You will not miss your financial goals for your child's college fund by missing one monthly contribution. You may consider foregoing a family vacation in order to save the money, but because of the long Time Horizon, you may decide you *can* take a vacation because you have a long time to make up for lost savings. Time Horizons help you compare your short-term goals with your long-term goals so you can make appropriate tradeoffs when necessary.

Looking at your *Really* Wants according to their Time Horizon can provide perspective as you go through your daily life in your organization. Here is a Time-Horizon exercise:

Step 1a – Write down the goals you wish to achieve by the end of your career.

Step 1b – Rank the goals you wish to achieve by the end of your career.

Step 2a – Write down the goals you wish to achieve by the end the year.

Step 2b – Rank the goals you wish to achieve by the end the year.

Step 3a – Write down goals you wish to achieve by the end each day.

Step 3b – Rank the goals you wish to achieve by the end each day.

Step 4 – Look at the Top 3 items on each list. Rank them in overall importance across all time horizons.

For Step 1, picture yourself on retirement day. What do you want to say you have accomplished? Do you want a certain position at work? Do you want your kids to be in college? Living at home? Do you want a comfortable retirement? A 401(k) with a certain amount of money? When you have thought of the goals you want by the end of your career, rank them in order of importance.

For Step 2, think of yourself at the end of this year. What do you want to say you have accomplished? Is there a particular project you want to complete? Is there a trip you wish to take with your family? Again, rank these goals in order of importance.

For Step 3, consider what you want at the end of each day. Do you want to feel like you accomplished something? Do you want to give your energy and focus to your family? Do you want to have the freedom at work to do things the way you want to do them? Rank these items in order of importance.

For Step 4, look at the top 3 items in each list (9 items in total). Rank them in order of importance. How does the project you want to finish by the end of the year compare with the trip you want to take or with the amount of money you want in your retirement fund?

When practicing SPACE, you must use your understanding of your *Really* Wants to contain your Self-Righteousness and avoid creating Heat. A situation may have little impact on your most important *Really* Wants, especially if they have a long Time Horizon. You must develop the ability to quickly determine how a situation affects your goals across various Time Horizons. If the immediate situation will not affect what you *really* want, you will find it easier to Center Your Ball and avoid creating Heat.

Bottom Lines

There will be times when you simply *cannot* give someone what they want. You may be asked to violate laws, ethics, or your own personal value system. For that reason, when you establish your *Really* Wants, you must also establish your Bottom Lines.

Your Bottom Lines are your core values which you will not violate under any circumstance. They become relevant when someone asks you to do something that violates those values. Bottom Lines run deeper than normal goals because they are rooted in your core beliefs. When faced with a Bottom Line, your values and beliefs create added pressure for you to meet that Bottom Line, increasing the likelihood that you will create Heat to meet a goal. Your Bottom Line may be that you will not do something that jeopardizes someone's safety. You may have a Bottom Line that you will not lie. Whatever your Bottom Line is, you must establish this clearly so, when placed in a difficult situation, you will know how to react.

When someone asks you to do something that violates one of your Bottom Lines, you will be put in a position where you will create Heat. You will either be disregarding a request or refusing to participate in an effort. It will reduce the size of your box and have other negative consequences. A situation which could violate one of your Bottom Lines is a very serious situation that requires you to stand up for things that are important to you.

The Challenger Disaster and Bottom Lines

The tragic explosion of the Space Shuttle Challenger in 1984 demonstrates the impact of Bottom Lines in difficult situations. To summarize, in January, NASA held a pre-launch review with its contractors to determine if there would be any problems launching the Space Shuttle in unusually cold temperatures. During the review, engineers at Morton-Thiokol expressed reservations about launching the Shuttle in the morning's cold temperature of 29°F. Data from a previous flight at 53°F showed erosion of the Solid Rocket Boosters' o-rings. The Thiokol engineers were concerned that the morning's unusually cold temperatures could be a significant problem for the o-rings.

There was enormous pressure to launch the Shuttle on the morning of January 28. There had already been two delays, the Vice President of the United States was attending the launch, and there was a high-profile guest flying on the mission. When Thiokol suggested that launching at the current temperature was unsafe, NASA pointedly expressed their frustration with Thiokol and accused them of changing the launch specifications the night before a launch. Pressure came from within Thiokol to approve the launch above reservations regarding safety. A senior executive at Thiokol told his Engineering Vice President to "take off your engineering hat and put on your management hat."[1]

On a conference call, Thiokol engineers were given a final chance to voice their reservations and delay the launch. In a tense moment, the engineers chose not to voice their concerns and Thiokol gave NASA the approval to launch. We all know how the story ended.

Here is an example of facing a Bottom Line. A Bottom Line for an engineer working on rocket boosters may be safety. If that engineer determines that safety is their Bottom Line, they simply will not agree to a situation where safety is inappropriately compromised.

What will happen to a person who holds to their Bottom Line? In the case of the Challenger explosion, if the engineer had held to a Bottom Line of safety, he would have been in a no-win situation. If he had objected to the launch and caused a delay, he would likely receive retaliation in some form. He might be removed from his current project, demoted, or possibly even fired. He would likely never again appear in a launch readiness review. Finally, he probably would never have known for sure if he was right. If the launch was delayed, the Shuttle would likely have been successfully launched on a warmer day. The engineer's management would suppose that he was worried about something that was not truly a problem.

If the engineer did not hold to a Bottom Line of safety, the Shuttle could be destroyed (it was), lives could be lost (they were), and the engineer would likely experience negative effects on his career. The engineer would have lost this battle either way. Unfortunately, by not holding to a Bottom Line of safety, seven astronauts also lost their lives.

[1] Hearings Before The Subcommittee On Science, Technology, And Space Committee On Commerce, Of The Science, And Transportation United States Senate Ninety-Ninth Congress Second Session On Space Shuttle Accident And The Rogers Commission Report - February 18, June 10 And 17, 1986, p.85

The Challenger explosion is an extreme case, but it demonstrates the difficult situation of facing a Bottom Line. When you are put in a Bottom Line situation, you must do what you can to minimize damage to yourself. Refuse an unreasonable request politely. Stick to facts and try to minimize emotion where possible. However, if you determine something is a Bottom Line, you must hold to it so you can sleep soundly knowing you made the right decision for you.

Beware of Short Time Horizons

Time Horizons are useful for providing perspective when you are in a situation where your Self-Righteousness is elevated. They enable you to recognize that what you think you want in the short term may not be what you *really* want in the long term. They help you accept the frustration with a situation and Center Your Ball. When the time horizon for a goal is short, you are more likely to act out of Self-Righteousness and create Heat.

When you think you must have something *now* or *today*, you elevate its importance relative to your other *Really* Wants. If you think "I *must* finish this report *today*," you will likely push hard to achieve that goal. If those efforts involve creating Heat with your coworkers or superiors, you will be more likely to do so if you feel pressured by an approaching deadline. This demonstrates that focusing on very short Time Horizons causes you to act out of Self-Righteousness and create Heat. This is why Time Horizons are so valuable: they help you ensure that even your short-term goals are SPACEable so you can avoid creating Heat.

Note that Bottom Lines are essentially Time Horizons of zero time. That is, a Bottom Line is something you absolutely must have at that instant. When you push back against a Bottom Line, you *will* Create Heat. When considering goals you think you *really* want, remember that the shorter the Time Horizon, the more likely you are to mistake that goal for a Bottom Line and create Heat to get it. Creating Heat will ultimately keep you from getting what you *really* want.

Integrity and Being Right – Finer Points of Self-Righteousness

There are finer points of Self-Righteousness which will help you avoid creating Heat.

First, there is a difference between Self-Righteousness and integrity. You may disagree with something someone wants you to do. For instance, if you are confident that a manager is misusing data and information, you will likely believe the manager is acting 'wrongly.' You must understand that, by complying with that manager's requests to develop reports and process information, you are following direction from someone above you in your organization. Though you may disagree with your management's decisions, you must still follow them (unless they violate your Bottom Lines). Following direction you disagree with is simply part of the Low Level of Pain expected in a High-Friction Organization. If you resist your management's request, you will simply create Heat, which will shrink your box and keep you from getting what you *really* want. If the manager truly has an integrity problem, you cannot, unfortunately, fix that problem. Your organization has chosen and entrusted your manager to run its operations, and your organization must address this manager's integrity problem. When you follow orders from your manager which do not violate your Bottom Lines, any lack of integrity lies with your manager. Attempting to solve your manager's integrity issues is Self-Righteousness. It will only create Heat and keep you from increasing the size of your box, which will limit your ability to do things that are beneficial for your organization.

Second, Self-Righteousness does not provide any real value to you when you get it. What is the value of being right? If you are *right* but you have a small box (and, therefore, little maneuvering room to make positive change), being *right* has not helped you get what you *really* want. Look again at your list of *Really* Wants. Is 'being right' on any of your Time Horizons? If it is, how well does that help you achieve any of your other *Really* Wants? The only value of being right is that it satisfies your personal ego or other psychological need at the expense of progress towards more tangible goals that make you better off in the long run.

Remember, acting out of Self-Righteousness will do nothing but create Heat and keep you from getting what you *really* want.

Assess-Accept-Act – The Other Two Parts

You have seen many facets of Self-Righteousness and how detrimental it is to achieving what you *really* want. You understand SPACEable goals and Time Horizons. By now, you should have a good idea about what you *really* want. Here are the two easy steps: Accept and Act.

Accept

You have put significant energy into figuring out what you *really* want. Review at your list: those are the things which are important to you in your life. Those items motivate you to get up every morning and drive to work. To achieve those goals, you must *accept* them as important goals that are worth working for. They are yardsticks by which you can measure individual situations and determine how you must act to get what you *really* want. You have heard many people say that, in organizations, you must "pick your battles." *Accept* ensures that you organize your life around what you truly value. When you are asked to do something which elevates your Self-Righteousness, you now only need to return to your list and see how the current situation affects what you *really* want. True *acceptance* of your *Really* Wants will help you contain your Self-Righteousness. When you *accept* that what you *really* want is important, you will find that more of your energy will be converted into Useful Work and channeled towards what is important to you.

Act

This is the simplest step of all. Once you have *Assessed* and *Accepted*, you simply need to *Act* according to what you *really* want. You have your list. You understand Self-Righteousness. You know how to pick your battles. You have a finite amount of energy available within your life. To get what you *really* want, simply ensure that you focus your energy towards what you *really* want instead of towards things which do not help you achieve your goals, like Self-Righteousness.

You can always choose to create Heat. If you choose to create Heat, it will simply keep you from getting what you *really* want.

Example: Personal SPACE
Riding Go-Carts with Brothers

Bryant	**Alex**
Engineer	Brother

On one of his few weekends off of work from AirSPACE, Bryant traveled to Long Island to attend a family wedding. Two of his brothers and his parents met him for the weekend. On Saturday morning, Bryant, his brothers, and his father decided to race go-carts. Bryant's father rode in the passenger's seat and his brother Douglas rode in the back seat as Bryant drove the rental car to a hotel to pick up their oldest brother, Alex.

At the hotel, Alex climbed into the back seat and said to Bryant: "Now we're not in a hurry to go anywhere." Bryant interpreted this statement to mean: "You don't have to speed." Bryant immediately felt Self-Righteous about Alex's statement, so he said: "Are you telling me how to drive in *my* car?" But he let the incident blow over as they started on their way to the racetrack.

Now Bryant expected that Alex knew the directions to the racetrack but it quickly became apparent that he did not. Alex would give directions from the back seat, which Bryant would follow. After a few turns, Bryant suggested they stop and ask for directions. Alex said: "No, I know where we're going." After a few more tentative turns, Bryant again suggested they stop, but Alex gave a similar response.

Bryant felt he was at a point of decision. He was driving the car, so he could certainly go where he wanted; if he wanted to stop and ask for directions, he had full control to do so. Then he thought about what he *really* wanted. Did he *really* want to ride go-carts? He did, but it was not his primary goal. He realized he was happy just being in the car with his two brothers and his father. He realized he just wanted to be with them in a peaceful environment. He would be just as happy if they drove around Long Island for four hours and never rode go-carts at all. Next, Bryant considered the effect of stopping to ask for directions. It would only create Heat with Alex and that would keep Bryant from getting what he *really* wanted. Then Bryant thought about the fact that he was receiving direction from the back seat from someone who did not know where they were going. He felt a bit Self-Righteous about that, but he recognized it as just that: Self-Righteousness. He decided to center his ball and go exactly where Alex told him to go.

Eventually, they arrived at the racetrack, raced go-carts, and had a great time. It took them a long time to get there. Bryant remembered driving down a dead end street after he had decided to center his ball and follow directions. He realized that, by simply following directions, he was getting *more* of what he *really* wanted; he was spending even more time driving with his family than he had expected. Everybody won in that situation. Bryant did not create Heat. He did not upset Alex (and it would have been unnecessary, since racing go-carts was not what he *really* wanted in this situation). By using Assess-Accept-Act in real-time and containing his Self-Righteousness, Bryant was able to use SPACE in a family situation to create an outcome that worked best for everyone involved.

Conclusions for Assess-Accept-Act

Remember these key points about Assess-Accept-Act:

- Your own goals are important.
- Your own goals are your yardstick for understanding where to focus your energy. You must ensure that you are channeling your energy towards your *Really* Wants.
- Hold your *Really* Wants up to the three criteria (attainable, elemental, free of Self-Righteousness) to ensure they are SPACEable.
- Knowing your own *Really* Wants and understanding your Bottom Lines enables you to sleep soundly knowing that you are holding to your core values.
- Remember the optimal operating location – Center Your Ball!
- Be careful about satisfying your Self-Righteousness – being *right* for the sake of being right will only keep you from getting what you *really* want.

Assess - Conclusions

Your behaviors are ultimately shaped by whether you are getting what you *really* want. When you get what you *really* want, it is easy to keep your energy from turning into Heat. It is easy to work to create win-win solutions. Most importantly, it is easy to give others what they *really* want.

When you are not getting what you *really* want, you will feel an underlying frustration. Your frustration will lead to actions and behaviors which your organization will not appreciate, value, or reward. You cannot begin to create a successful interface with your organization until you are clear about what you *really* want.

Understanding what you *really* want enables you to pick your battles. It also enables you to avoid acting out of Self-Righteousness and devoting your energy to pursuits that are not really important to you. Your key to creating SPACE is a thorough understanding of what you *really* want.

Example: AirSPACE

Tool Shop Utilization Report

Assess Implications

Andrew
Supervisor

|

Bryant
Engineer

Bryant thought about how he was feeling about the one-page report. He knew he was frustrated with what Andrew was asking him to do. He thought things like "this isn't right!" and "this isn't fair!" He was upset that Andrew did not even acknowledge the great work that he did. He felt disregarded from a technical standpoint *and* from a personal standpoint.

Bryant recognized these thoughts as Self-Righteousness. No, it wasn't *right*, but Andrew was behaving consistently with behaviors that AirSPACE has indicated were acceptable. Andrew took a deep breath, thought of his kids playing in the park last night, and centered his ball.

Bryant thought again about what he really wanted. He knew that he *really* wanted to help his wife provide a good living for themselves and their kids. He *really* wanted to come home at night with energy to give to his family. Did he *really* want acknowledgement from Andrew? Sure, he wanted that. However, when he compared that to anything involving his family, it was not so important.

Did Bryant *really* want this one-page report? The report was a reflection on his skill and intelligence. It ultimately did not have anything to do with his wife and kids and getting home at a reasonable time in the evening. If he thought honestly, it would probably be quicker to develop the report the way Andrew wanted than to collect all the data every month to do it the 'right' way. Bryant was not comfortable with Andrew's request. Nevertheless, when Bryant held the situation up to Organizational Mechanics, what AirSPACE and Andrew *really* wanted, and the things he *really* wanted, his version of the report was really not that important.

Key Points from Assess:

1) Acting out of Self-Righteousness will only keep you from getting what you *really* want.

2) The Goals-Righteousness Model shows that the optimal operating location in a High-Friction Organization is to Center Your Ball.

3) Self-Righteousness sets up lose-lose solutions and is, by definition, narrow-minded.

4) Learn to recognize your Self-Righteousness so you can contain it before it leads you to create Heat.

5) Use Assess-Accept-Act to determine and get what you *really* want.

6) Ensure that what you *really* want is SPACEable; that is, Attainable, Elemental, and free of Self-Righteousness. If you choose goals that are Non-SPACEable, they will lead you to create Heat.

7) Consider Time Horizons when reflecting on what you *really* want.

8) Know your Bottom Lines so you can be prepared to act decisively in extreme situations.

You now have the information you need to tune your interface in a way that your organization will appreciate. Organizations and the people within them simply want to get what they *really* want. You know how to uncover what people *really* want by observing their behavior. You also have a good understanding of what you *really* want. You are better equipped than ever to choose your battles. You know where you want to focus your valuable energy and what is not important. Now you are ready to learn the rules for developing an interface that any organization, especially a High-Friction Organization, will appreciate.

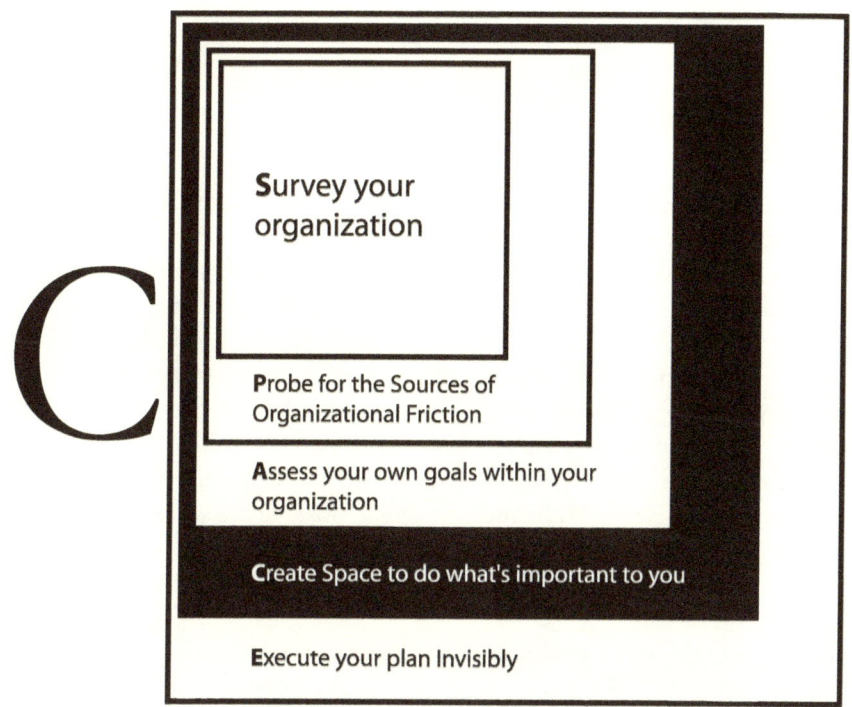

C

To get what you *really* want at work, you must properly adjust your interface with your organization. It is not intuitive or natural for most people to work in organizations without creating Heat. Fortunately, there is a straightforward way to tune your interface so you deliver your work in a way that your organization will appreciate.

Create SPACE explains the behaviors that are the keys to success in any organization, especially High-Friction organizations. There is nothing wrong with you or your goals, thoughts and ideas. However, there may be changes you can make to your style – your *interface* with your organization – which will make your organization appreciate the *way* you do your job in addition to the great job you already do. Create SPACE describes those style modifications that will improve your interface with your organization.

Create SPACE will show you how to work in a way that avoids creating Heat, enables you to increase the size of your box and, ultimately, helps you get what you *really* want. The Create SPACE chapter will:

• Introduce *Invisibility*, a condition in which some members of an organization are *allowed*, in the organization's eyes, to ignore others.

- Explore the eight Laws of Invisibility, the ways to work within an organization without creating Heat.

Invisibility

Everyone has seen someone rocket up the corporate ladder. What sets these people apart from everyone else? They naturally work without creating Heat. That is not to say they do not challenge people or work to fix problems within the organization; they do these things. They simply do them in ways that do not create Heat. SPACE Creators naturally understand a key topic in this section: the concept of Invisibility. Invisibility is a condition that exists in High-Friction Organizations. It creates a structure which you feel every day but cannot see; because you cannot see it, you do not know it is there until someone tells you about it. You must understand Invisibility so you can work in a way that does not create Heat. To define Invisibility, observe life at AirSPACE to see Invisibility in action.

Example: AirSPACE

Invisibility

Bryant
Engineer

The AirSPACE corporate mission statement reads: "People are our most valued asset." Because AirSPACE is a High-Friction Organization, what the company *says* it values is sometimes different than what it values in practice. AirSPACE does make an earnest effort to learn how its employees are feeling about their jobs and their organization. AirSPACE sends out an annual survey called the Employee Morale Assessment (the "EMA") to all employees to gauge morale, stress-level, and general attitudes. All managers in AirSPACE are told that the survey results will be included as a measure on their performance reviews and they should focus a portion of their job on improving those results.

When the results are less than favorable, a department convenes a task force to better understand the problem. The task force is made up of the department's management and non-management employees and is created to connect with employees who filled out the survey, learn why they answered the survey negatively, and make recommendations for improvement.

Bryant was called to a meeting to review his department's EMA results. The department manager reviewed each page of the survey results with everyone. The results showed that morale was suffering because people felt like they were unable to balance their work and home life. So the department manager asked for volunteers to participate in a work-life improvement task force and develop actions to enhance work-life balance. Bryant wanted to help, so he volunteered. Three other managers in the department also volunteered to participate in the task force, leaving Bryant as the only non-management employee on the team.

Bryant walked into the first meeting and sat down. One manager handed out a printout of the EMA questions that related to work-life balance. She read each of the questions aloud, then said to everyone: "You know, this survey is really poorly written." The other managers nodded and she continued. "The questions are really confusing. It looks like you could easily answer 'yes' when you mean 'no.'" The other managers joined in and, for the next five minutes, they all discussed the survey's shortcomings.

After that part of the conversation, one of the managers said: "Since we're on this task force, let's assume there actually *is* a problem with work-life balance. What should we do?" Another answered: "Let's hold focus groups with the employees in the department, review the questions, and ask what those questions meant to them. That way, we can begin to understand, specifically, what they think the problem is." Good idea, thought Bryant, as he continued to listen. The manager continued: "Let's divide the department into four groups, since there are four of us, and we'll each lead our own individual group."

Bryant immediately felt uncomfortable. He recognized the problem with work-life balance – there were some managers who were very demanding of their employees. They made it known they were unhappy if their employees worked less than 11 hours a day. They would frequently give their employees assignments which were to be finished immediately, regardless of what they were working on. The employee had to drop everything, work on this new project, and still get their normal job completed, regularly resulting in late hours. Bryant felt that some on the management team were contributors to the problem of work-life balance. If those same managers were leading the focus groups, employees would not feel free to speak their true thoughts.

Bryant decided to voice his concern. He said, carefully: "If there was a problem with work-life balance, it's possible that it may be impacted by how employees in this department receive assignments and direction. Since management decides how to distribute work, some employees may not feel comfortable giving candid feedback on work-life balance when managers are present. I suggest that management not be present at the focus groups so everyone in the room will feel comfortable giving their true feedback."

None of the other managers in the room spoke while Bryant was speaking. They did not interrupt him and they sat patiently while he made his point. However, when he was done, the managers picked up exactly where they had left off. Without comment, they began to divide the department into four focus groups, which would be led by each person in the room. It was as if Bryant had not even spoken. Nobody argued with Bryant's point, nor did they even acknowledge it. They simply acted as if he had not given any input. Bryant felt like it did not matter that he was even in the room. Bryant felt *I*nvisible.

Of course, Bryant is not invisible. His managers do not try to sit in his chair when he is in it. They do not bump into him as he is walking down the hallway. Managers in his department greet him in the morning and they speak to him throughout their day. There are times, however, (like in this work-life balance meeting) when they treat him as if he is Invisible. So, Bryant is not *i*nvisible to his managers, but he is clearly *I*nvisible to his managers.

> **Invisibility** - You are Invisible to someone if they can choose to ignore you and not suffer any negative personal consequences in the organization.

Is Bryant "*Invisible*" to his managers according to the above definition? Of course he is. What happens to the managers if they disregard his input? Nothing will happen to them, aside from not receiving all of Bryant's best ideas. They will proceed to hold their focus groups. They may not get the real information about why employees believe there is a problem with work-life balance. However, none of the managers in the room will be hurt or reprimanded by ignoring Bryant's input. This is daily life at AirSPACE: Bryant gives input in meetings to his managers, but they can disregard his input without suffering any negative personal consequences.

Consider the situation in reverse. Can Bryant ignore his manager's input and ideas? He can, of course, but not without negative consequences. If he ignores his manager's input, he may be given a lower performance review, tedious tasks, or be otherwise marginalized. Bryant will suffer negative consequences if he inappropriately challenges or ignores his management's ideas. Therefore, Bryant is Invisible to his management.

Being **V**isible is the opposite of being **I**nvisible. You are **V**isible to others if you *can* ignore their ideas and not suffer any negative personal consequences in the organization. Bryant is **I**nvisible to his managers. Bryant's managers are **V**isible to him.

How does Invisibility impact Bryant's choices of how to respond to his managers in the EMA task force meeting? Bryant could push his point. He could say: "Didn't you hear me? If you really want to solve the problems in this department, you cannot be present when the focus groups are held." He could push his point until someone acknowledged his input. What would happen then? Bryant has seen this many times before at AirSPACE. He has seen people who were Invisible act as if they were Visible. He has seen people push their points in meetings when management clearly had their minds set on a particular course of action. When an employee was overaggressive in making a point, that employee's manager received a phone call. Their manager was asked to 'keep their employee in line' and to 'make sure their employee behaves.' The employee would then receive 'coaching' from his manager on appropriate behavior. Over time, if the employee continued to behave in this way, they would feel negative consequences in the form of exclusion from projects and negative comments on performance reviews.

You must understand Invisibility to avoid creating Heat and increase the size of your box. Invisibility is closely linked to Heat Creation. Since you now understand Invisibility, Heat Creation can be defined in the context of Invisibility:

> ## You create Heat when you are Invisible but you act as if you are Visible.

High-Friction Organizations hate Heat. If you wish to avoid creating Heat, you must understand Invisibility. When you are Invisible to someone, you must not act as if you are Visible. *This is the foundation for the Laws of Invisibility.* If you act Visibly towards someone to whom you are Invisible, you will create Heat. Your box will get smaller and you will not get what you *really* want. Act Invisibly when you are Invisible and you will not create Heat. When you use your Invisibility to give your organization what it *really* wants, your organization will reward you.

Practicing the Laws of Invisibility does not mean that you avoid voicing opinions or challenging others appropriately. It does not mean that you walk around with your head down, always bending to others' decisions. It *does* mean that you must recognize that some people within your organization can ignore your ideas; this is simply part of the physics of High-Friction Organizations. Consequently, you must deliver your ideas accordingly. Practicing the Laws of Invisibility means you cannot assume that others *must* listen to you or acknowledge your input. You must frequently find other options for getting what you want when someone who is Visible to you rejects your ideas. Notice the link between Invisibility and Organizational Mechanics: because of Friction and Invisibility, less Useful Work will be accomplished because you are frequently forced to use multiple approaches to get something done.

Nobody wants to admit that they are Invisible. It doesn't *feel* good and it doesn't *feel* right. Countless seminars and books are based on the basic assumption that you are valuable and, with persistence and motivation, you are capable of making great improvements to your organization. While SPACE does not suggest that one person cannot change the world, SPACE *does* suggest that people can be ignored in High-Friction Organizations. Invisibility is a disappointing reality which is part of the physics of working in a High-Friction Organization. It is responsible for endless frustration, burn-out, and apathy of workers. Invisibility is especially frustrating because it is an unseen stumbling block. It is like a hidden tripwire that is always placed across your path. You continue to trip over it but you do not see the obstacle. Over time, you become frustrated because you do not know why you cannot walk without tripping.

Invisibility is as much a fact of life as Friction within an organization. Just as most employees cannot change the Friction level, they cannot change the Invisibility structure. Accepting this Invisibility is part of the Low Level of Pain that comes with working in a High-Friction Organization. It is not right or comfortable to accept that you can be ignored. It is certainly difficult to smile and maintain a positive attitude when someone is treating you as if you do not exist.

Invisibility, while a disappointing fact of life, is a key to success within your organization. When you understand Invisibility, you can explain why some colleagues are so successful: they understand and accept their Invisibility and act accordingly in the presence of Visible people. They set their interface so they act Invisibly when appropriate. Invisibility implies that, because you are not *seen* in certain situations, you can operate below radar screens. When you begin to consider the possibilities that arise from operating below radar screens, many exciting opportunities appear which you may not have considered. You will find you have many more options for accomplishing your objectives than you previously thought. As your learn the Laws of Invisibility, SPACE follows the perspective: "You're Invisible – so use this Invisibility to your advantage to get what you *really* want."

To be successful in your High Friction Organization, set your interface so you act Invisibly, especially when you are in the presence of people who are Visible to you. You do not need to change your *values*. You simply need to modify your *behaviors* so you work in a way which your organization appreciates. Now that you are aware of Invisibility, you are ready to learn the laws which guide how to operate effectively within your organization's Invisibility structure.

The Laws of Invisibility are your keys to success because they show you how to tune your interface and work without creating Heat.

The Laws of Invisibility

There are eight Laws of Invisibility. The Laws of Invisibility enable you to create SPACE and increase the size of your box. They tie together the entire SPACE process because they synthesize the earlier phases of SPACE into a cohesive strategy for success. You know about Friction. You know that people do not always want what they say that want. You know what is important to you. Now you are ready to deliver. Now you are ready to use Invisibility to give your organization what it *really* wants so you can get what you *really* want.

The Laws of Invisibility are like any other set of laws: each individual ultimately decides whether or not they will follow them. Laws can be broken and, sometimes, there are consequences for breaking laws. If you choose to break the Laws of Invisibility, you are simply choosing to behave in ways that create Heat, which will keep you from getting what you *really* want.

The Laws of Invisibility:

1) Use conciliation and detachment to create the necessary space between the system and you to do what is important.

2) Know that the world likes to keep turning; it does not like being disturbed.

3) Self-Righteousness is the enemy of Invisibility. There is a difference between doing the right thing and getting the right thing done. Do what works, not what you believe is right just because it is right.

4) Don't give people what they want; give them what they *really* want. Anticipate people's needs so you can give them what they *really* want.

5) Accept that Invisibility comes with a Low Level of Pain. Some energy will be wasted as Heat and Non-Useful Work.

6) Do not engage difficult people.

7) You will not get the credit you want. You must accept the credit you get.

8) Always remember your place as an Invisible person. Deference is necessary when you are Invisible. Bumping back is seldom successful.

Accept the truth of your Invisibility, and you will start down the path towards a bigger box. Commit to living an Invisible lifestyle by choosing to Center Your Ball instead of creating Heat. Always act Invisibly; that is, live according to the Laws of Invisibility. You will no longer create Heat and your box will grow.

The Laws of Invisibility – Law #1

> **Law #1:** Use conciliation and detachment to create the necessary space between the system and you to do what is important.

The first and most important Law of Invisibility is that you must operate in a way that enables you to increase your maneuvering room and flexibility so you can do what is important. Law #1 implies that the 'system' is always trying to close in around you. 'The system' is your immediate work area or your larger organization. It is the operating area within your organization which contains the Friction which you can rub against and create Heat. In a High Friction Organization, everyday forces get in the way of accomplishing Useful Work, frustrating your efforts to make meaningful change. As a result, it feels like the system is always trying to knock your Self-Righteousness ball off-center. You must always keep your ball centered to create SPACE so you have the breathing room – the freedom and maneuvering room – to do what you believe is important.

You create SPACE in two ways. First, you must perform actions that expand your box. Second, you must not behave in ways that *decrease* the size of your box. To expand your box, *always practice conciliation*. To avoid shrinking your box, *practice selective detachment* when something triggers your Self-Righteousness.

> **Conciliation** – *noun* – The act of gaining (as goodwill) by pleasing acts.
>
> - Merriam-Webster Dictionary
>
> **Conciliation** – "I can do that!"
>
> - SPACE Definition

Conciliation increases the size of your box. When you practice conciliation, you work to help people in a way that makes them appreciate you as a colleague. When you effectively practice conciliation, your colleagues will welcome you in any meeting room and on any project.

To employ conciliation, you must engrain the following four words into your memory: "I can do that!" Think about those four simple words. Isn't this what *everyone* wants their employees to say? Most people prefer colleagues who will not give them all the reasons why something *cannot* happen; rather, everyone wants a colleague who will earnestly try to satisfy their requests. This is the kind of manager, colleague, or employee that people want to work with on any team.

Imagine what life would be like if people did not put up so much resistance when asked to do something. Imagine what life would be like if people just said: "I can do that!" and then delivered.

Conciliation is *not* blind agreement. SPACE does *not* suggest you use these four words without the intention of following through. SPACE does not suggest that you be disingenuous when you agree to something. When you say: "I can do that!" you must intend to follow through. The SPACE strategy is about giving others what they *really* want so you can get what you *really* want. From Survey, you know that all work in a High Friction Organization will not be Useful Work. From Probe, you know that everyone in your organization does not act according to published corporate goals (they sometimes act very much against those goals). Probe also demonstrated that people do not always ask for what they *really* want. From Assess, you understand what you *really* want and your own Bottom Lines. When you put it all together, you will find there is very little you cannot agree to do for someone. SPACE does not suggest that you blindly follow orders. Yet if someone (especially someone who is Visible to you) asks you to do something which you *can* do for them, you should do it. Furthermore, if they have made up their mind that they want a particular thing done and it does not violate your Bottom Lines or keep you from getting what you *really* want, you should do it.

Why would you *not* give someone what they *really* want if it does not violate one of your Bottom Lines? You may resist requests because you do not believe that what you are asked to do is a good use of your time or talents. Perhaps you resist requests because you do not believe they are right for your organization. Remember Organizational Mechanics and Self-Righteousness. When you are a SPACE Creator, you recognize there are many different approaches to problems and *your* way is not the only way. You also recognize that not all of your work will be converted to Useful Work, so participating in Non-Useful Work is simply a part of life in your organization. When you consider the SPACE you can create by Centering Your Ball and giving someone what they *really* want, you will find there are very few times when you are unable to say: "I can do that."

Agreeing to something can give you a large amount of leeway. When you say: "I can do that," you gain the freedom to interpret what someone has requested. You can satisfy their request in the way you deem appropriate. As long as you deliver what the requester *really* wants, you can often use a request to do many things *you* believe are important. Even if you do not fully agree with what you are being asked, saying "I can do that" gives you time to consider different approaches for giving someone what they *really* want. Especially if the request knocks your ball off-center, "I can do that" gives you time to Center Your Ball and return to emotional equilibrium so you can think more clearly about a request. With more time, you can create more options to give someone what they *really* want and simultaneously get what you *really* want. With this extra time, you also make the opportunity to clarify your thoughts and develop follow-up questions about your assignment. You can use the follow-up questions to guide the requester along a path that works for you. More importantly, follow-up questions mean you can hold a follow-up meeting with someone who is usually higher than you in your organization. Why not use this as an opportunity to meet with your requester, ask follow-up questions, and show them you are the kind of person who wants to give them what they asked for? More time with your management is a good thing, especially when you keep your ball centered and give them what they *really* want.

Finally, as in the Tool Shop Utilization Report example, saying "I can do that" and agreeing to a request may be less painful than doing the job the way you consider to be 'right.' Sometimes, it may actually save time to do something the way you are asked to do it. With the goodwill you generate by saying "I can do that," you may free more time to work within your larger box.

Detachment – Emotionally Disengage Selectively

Success through SPACE hinges upon keeping your ball centered. You will not be able to graciously give someone what they *really* want if you are feeling frustrated or Self-Righteous. If you fail to keep your ball centered, you will lose the hard-won gains you earned through conciliation. To ensure that you reap the benefits of conciliation, practice selective *detachment* to avoid shrinking your box.

To practice selective detachment, you must be aware of your level of emotional engagement in a situation. Recall a time when you worked hard on a project and spent significant time and energy into making something good happen. Did anyone criticize your hard work and minimize your efforts in front of others? How did you feel about that? If "upset" or "angry" describes how you felt, you were 'emotionally engaged' in your project. It is at these times that detachment is critical to your success.

Detachment is, in SPACE terms, 'instant ball-centering.' Selective detachment is a trick of perspective when you are emotionally engaged. It takes practice, but it becomes easier over time and the benefits are enormous. You must learn, practice, and apply selective detachment to create SPACE. Selective detachment is not natural. It is natural for people to care about what they build and create. Telling yourself to detach emotionally from something you believe is important is not easy. How do you apply selective detachment? It is all about your perspective. Consider two types of perspective: absolute perspective and relative perspective.

For *absolute perspective*, consider your work in absolute terms within your life. Ask yourself: "What *is* work?" Work is a place that pays you to do a job. To reduce it to its simplest terms, you are a hired gun, paid to do something specific for your organization. Do you feel so passionately about your job that, if your organization asked you, you would give up your life for it?

Your work and your job are important. However, the place where you work was likely established before you arrived and it will likely be there after you leave. Through an absolute perspective, work is...work. Would you compare the loss of a project at work with the loss of a loved one? This perspective may help you Center Your Ball when you are faced with a situation that aggravates your Self-Righteousness. When crazy things happen which are explainable only by understanding the Friction in a situation, absolute perspective can help you see that what happens at work is not *so* important in the larger scheme of life. Work is worthy of an *appropriate* amount of emotional engagement. When crazy things happen at work, think of an absolute perspective and Center Your Ball.

For *relative perspective*, recall the Assess phase of SPACE. You spent time and energy figuring out what you *really* want. When you compare events that happen at work to what you *really* want and realize that those events do not prevent you from getting what you *really* want, it is easy to detach from emotionally charged situations. If you are in a difficult and emotional situation where you may create Heat, wouldn't you rather detach, avoid Heat Creation, and keep your box from shrinking? It is much easier to detach when you realize you will get what you *really* want, regardless of the outcome of the immediate situation.

You must, however, avoid crossing the line between detachment and apathy. *SPACE does not suggest that you become apathetic about your job.* Apathy does not help you *or* your organization meet your respective goals. You should certainly fight for things that are important to you. However, SPACE suggests you should not fight for something when your ball is off-center and you are engaged emotionally. When you are emotionally engaged, it is too easy to act out of Self-Righteousness and create Heat.

The Law of Conservation of Organizational Energy shows that there is loss and pain which you must accept when working in a High-Friction Organization. Because of Friction, you will feel *some* low level of Invisibility Pain. Detachment is part of that Low-Level of Pain you feel when working in a High-Friction

Organization. You want to be fully engaged in your work. You want success for your organization to the point that you feel loyalty and emotional engagement. You know that, in a perfect world, throwing your passion and emotional energy behind your work will improve the quality of your results. Your Low-Level of Pain is partially from the disappointment you feel when you recognize you cannot *always* be passionate about or emotionally engaged in your work because this will set yourself up for creating Heat. Detachment is uncomfortable because it does not feel 'right.' You may ask yourself: "Why must I withhold my emotional energy from my organization? Why must I behave like this?" The answer is: "because you are in a High-Friction Organization."

Detachment enables us to accept some crazy things that happen in High-Friction Organizations with a smile. If something catches you by surprise, detachment can ensure that you accept new information with humor and grace, which will be appreciated by your colleagues and managers.

Conciliation and detachment, together, are a winning combination for a bigger box at work. You will find that, over time, your stress level at work will diminish. It is less stressful to say: "I can do that!" than to state all the reasons why something cannot happen. You will feel less stress and frustration when you master detachment.

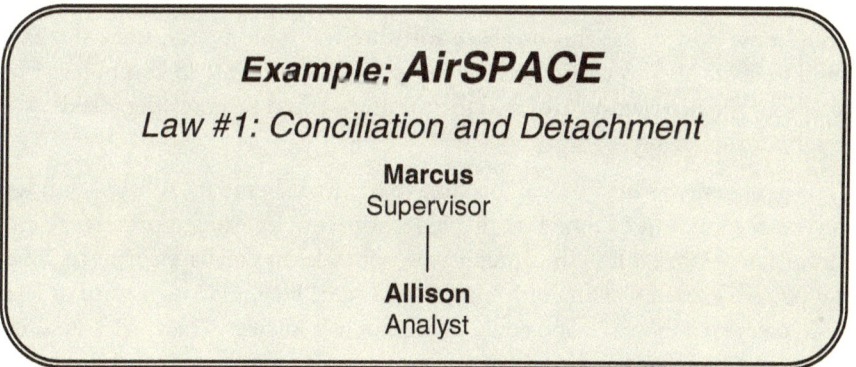

Allison was an analyst for AirSPACE. She was instructed to record data on how often equipment within the Engine Production Facility (EPF) was broken down. Allison was a motivated and loyal AirSPACE employee. She worked hard to make good things happen. Allison also understood Organizational Mechanics and was a well-practiced SPACE Creator. She knew how to make good things happen in a way that her organization appreciated.

Create Space

Marcus, Allison's supervisor, was a confirmed Point Source of Friction. Marcus was comfortable with AirSPACE's negative attitude towards subordinates. He would seldom ask his subordinates for input on matters that affected them. He would also make major changes to job functions without prior communication.

Unlike other supervisors in the EPF, Marcus did not have a college degree. Because of his age and family situation, he would never go back to school to earn a degree. As such, he resolved to stay in his current job and benefit from the perks and pay of his position as much as he could. Marcus passed along busy-work assignments to Allison, then spent most of his day in his office with the door closed. Allison quickly became accustomed to receiving a steady stream of Non-Useful Work from Marcus.

Allison spent a bit of time in the production area of AirSPACE's EPF. She noticed that the facility was not effective at managing its inventory of engine components. Sometimes there would not be enough parts available and the facility would not be able to build the engines its customers requested. Also, the EPF kept an enormous quantity of other parts which never seemed to be used. Allison recognized that AirSPACE was losing a lot of money because of the EPF's mismanagement of inventory.

Allison began thinking about this problem and came up with a solution. She could develop an inventory management program using available database software to solve the EPF's inventory management problem. The fact that she did not know how to use this database software was a motivator, since she had wanted to learn how to write database programs. The EPF had computers throughout the production area and the program could be easily deployed throughout the facility.

The problem was how to sell this idea to her management. Allison's job was to record the amount of time that machines were not working, not to solve inventory problems. Her job certainly was not to learn database software. She could picture herself walking into Marcus's office: "Hey, Marcus: I want to learn how to create databases." She could hear Marcus's answer: "Hey, Allison: Get back to your machines and take your data like you're supposed to." However, since Allison was a shrewd SPACE Creator, she determined that the best approach was to work Invisibly and develop the program in her spare time. She would create SPACE and use her increased SPACE and maneuvering room to carry out her plan. What was her strategy? Conciliation and detachment.

Allison practiced conciliation whenever Marcus would deliver an assignment. Allison would always smile whenever Marcus gave her an assignment and say: "Sure, I can do that." Even when Marcus asked her to make seemingly superfluous charts or minor and tedious changes to a management presentation,

Allison cheerfully agreed to Marcus's requests and quickly completed them. Instead of delivering her assignment to Marcus immediately upon completion, Allison rewarded herself by spending some time learning how to use the database software. She would always deliver her work to Marcus thoroughly completed and in a timely manner. Marcus, satisfied with Allison's work, was happy to spend time in his closed office.

Allison also practiced detachment in order to keep her ball centered. Sometimes the assignments from Marcus were mind-boggling. Marcus had lost a computer file of a 10-page report. Since he had the printed copy, he asked Allison to retype the report. This was a request that really annoyed Allison. She initially felt indignant that she would be asked to use her versatile skills to retype a 10-page report. That job was going to cost her a full day of work. Allison quickly adjusted her perspective and asked how this impacted what she *really* wanted. She *really* wanted to go back to her database software instruction manual and learn programming. She recognized this would just set her back a day. Marcus would be happy to have the report retyped as he requested. Allison's box would get a little bigger if she cheerfully accepted the assignment without complaining. So she did.

It was not long before Allison had learned how to write programs with the database software and was ready to create the inventory management program. Allison spent a lot of time with the workers in the production area to understand exactly what they needed in the program. She developed the program, produced a prototype, ran a pilot, fixed the bugs, deployed the computer program, and held training sessions for the production workers. The computer program was a huge success and Allison noted, with satisfaction, that the EPF was meeting its production targets better since the program was implemented.

What did Allison get out of this? She got a new and valuable skill on her resume: database programming. She also got a resume line-item about the money-saving implementation of the inventory management program. Finally, she developed wonderful friendships with the people who used the program every day.

What *didn't* Allison get? Not surprisingly, she *didn't* get a thank-you from Marcus. Inventory control was outside of Marcus's job responsibilities and he did not pay much attention to what happened in other areas of the EPF. So Allison did not get any official recognition for her work and effort.

The real impact of Allison's SPACE Creation hit her when she decided to move out of the state and leave AirSPACE. Allison's going-away lunch was the best-attended lunch that the EPF had held in recent memory. The production workers contributed to buy her some very nice going-away presents and a goodbye card that was full of touching personal messages. Allison used conciliation and detachment to create SPACE. She did the Non-Useful Work that she knew was just part of life in a High-Friction Organization. With her bigger box, she put her efforts into something she found useful. And she benefited in ways that she had not expected when she started the project.

The Laws of Invisibility – Law #2

Law #2: Know that the world likes to keep turning; it does not like being disturbed.

People do not enjoy hearing about or dealing with problems they believe others should solve on their own. Law #2 states that people would rather their worlds continue to turn in peace and harmony without problems or difficulty. To ensure you create SPACE and are viewed as an asset in your management's eyes, you must do what you can to be a versatile problem solver. You must keep problems which should be solved by you and your colleagues off of your management's radar screen unless you are unable to solve them *and* your organization will suffer negative consequences if you do not escalate the problem. When you are Invisible, you must ensure that, for the Visible people around you, their worlds keep turning peacefully.

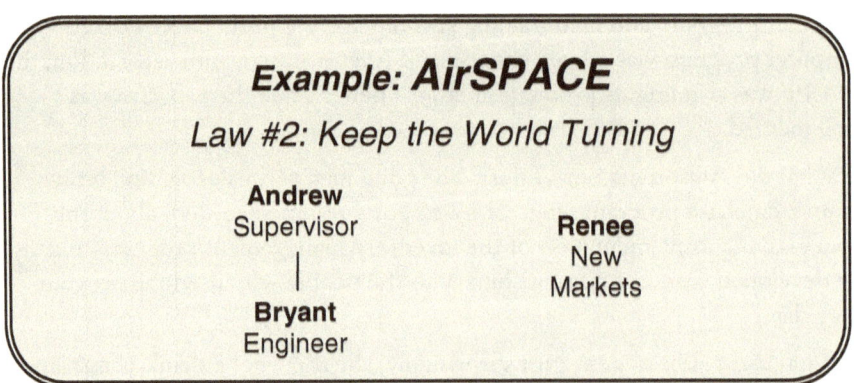

Example: *AirSPACE*

Law #2: Keep the World Turning

Andrew
Supervisor

Renee
New
Markets

Bryant
Engineer

AirSPACE recently opened a facility in the Czech Republic. In a high level AirSPACE meeting, a Vice-President asked for an in-depth review of the new facility's manufacturing processes. The assignment filtered down to Andrew, who passed it along to Bryant. Bryant needed to find someone in AirSPACE who could help get the information from the Czech Republic. AirSPACE has a New Markets group whose staff regularly travels to all AirSPACE facilities. The

New Markets group is the liaison between AirSPACE's main facilities and satellite plants. They are also responsible for ensuring that technical expertise is shared effectively among all facilities.

Sometimes it is difficult to get the New Markets group to gather requested information. They had a reputation within AirSPACE for being unresponsive and uncooperative. While the staff of the New Markets group frequently traveled to all of the facilities, they were not always approachable when asked to gather information.

Bryant first located Renee, the engineer in the New Markets group who travels to the Czech Republic. He needed to convince Renee to collect the data required for the in-depth review of the facility and to write the preliminary report. Even though this was Renee's job, Bryant expected that Renee might be uncooperative and it might be difficult to convince her to satisfy his request.

Bryant called Renee and, as expected, it was not a smooth process to get what he needed. First, there were currently no trips scheduled to the Czech Republic. Second, there were already some requests made to the New Markets group for information from the Czech facility. Any additional requests would be put at the bottom of the queue. In a passing conversation, Bryant told Andrew that it might be difficult to get New Markets to develop the report. Andrew said: "Just give it another try and, if you can't get someone to work on it, we'll just report to the Vice President that we couldn't get New Markets to get us the information. But get some documentation, like an e-mail, from them saying they can't get us what we need." Clearly, Bryant thought, Andrew was trying to ensure that someone else was ultimately held responsible if the report was not completed.

Bryant called Renee again and, again, Renee indicated she was unsure whether she would be able to get the report to him in the near future. Unfortunately, Bryant could not get Renee to document her reasons for not generating the report. Bryant considered his options. Andrew did not seem very concerned about this assignment. In their conversations about this project, Andrew indicated that he did not see a lot of value in it and would be willing to say "We can't do it" if it were too difficult. Bryant recognized that pursuing this issue further with Renee would probably go nowhere. He was very close to telling Andrew they should just close out the assignment and say it was too difficult to get the report.

Bryant thought about the Laws of Invisibility. Law #2 states that people like their world to keep turning. If you are Invisible to someone, you will create the most SPACE if you bring them fewer problems and more solutions. So Bryant came up with another option. He thought about what Renee *really* wanted. He had heard the labels that his colleagues used for the New Market group:

"uncooperative, unresponsive, useless." These labels reminded him that this group may be a Source of Friction and that he needed to Probe deeper to understand other people's motivations. What did the New Market group *really* want? He knew that everyone in that group traveled an enormous amount and did not spend much time at any single facility. He knew that they dealt daily with airport delays, missed meals, and living out of suitcases. He expected that *he* would feel annoyed at the barrage of requests which always seemed to come in. If *he* were in Renee's job, he would probably just want people to keep their requests to themselves. Bryant thought it would be useful if he made his request as painless as possible and showed Renee that he understood and respected her situation. So he outlined the report which he wanted Renee to create. He wrote it out so all Renee needed to do was fill out very specific information. He spent an hour reviewing whatever documentation he could find on the Czech facility and, in doing so, developed a list of three people whom Renee would need to contact during a visit. He sent her the report outline along with the contact phone numbers of those three people. To his surprise and pleasure, Renee replied with a note thanking him for the report preparation. She said that a trip was just scheduled and she would see to it that the report was completed.

What happened here? Bryant was about to give up on an assignment which he and his supervisor thought was non-value-added. Instead, he gave one additional, final effort to make the report happen. He sensed the presence of a Source of Friction and Probed deeply to understand what others *really* want. His creativity and persistence enabled him to tell Andrew that the report would be on his desk in two weeks. Andrew was pleased that he got what he asked for. More importantly, Andrew got what he wanted without having to be involved in any of the challenge and uncertainty that Bryant faced. Instead of bothering Andrew with the play-by-play drama of the effort, Bryant just gracefully reported to Andrew: "I have agreement from New Markets to complete the report in two weeks." Bryant's box got a little bigger through this experience.

Keep Their World Turning

Very few people enjoy obstacles that needlessly take up their time and keep them from getting what they want. People who are Visible to you do not like to hear "no" to something they want. Your organization hired you to handle problems when you can handle them. It pays you to make things happen. It did not hire you to tell why you *cannot* do something. Especially in High-Friction Organizations, when a Visible person gives an Invisible person an assignment, the Visible person does not want to hear excuses or reasons why things cannot be done. They just want it done. They ultimately want their world to keep turning in undisturbed peace.

In an ideal world, management is available to remove roadblocks to progress and success. In High-Friction Organizations, there are simply more of those roadblocks to overcome. A larger amount of Non-Useful work is endemic to the organization. SPACE Creators must recognize the difference between a roadblock and a hurdle. You can jump over a hurdle. It is much more difficult to get through a roadblock.

In High-Friction Organizations, it is difficult to tell the difference between a hurdle and a roadblock. If there are negative attitudes towards subordinates or functional chimneys, others within the organization will be less inclined to help you meet your goals. These Sources of Friction create more resistance to getting work done. Because of all the Non-Useful Work in High-Friction Organizations, people become concerned that they are not doing their job effectively when things take far longer to accomplish than they think they should. This resistance and Non-Useful Work usually does not *prevent* work from being accomplished if you are creative about making things happen. Even in High-Friction Organizations, there are very few true roadblocks.

Your management should be informed of problems you cannot solve which will negatively impact your organization. However, your managers ultimately want you to solve the problems you can solve so they are not involved when they do not need to be. You may be able to think of many potential problems for anything you are asked to do. Those who are Visible to you will be happiest when they are not consulted regarding everything that could possibly go wrong.

To embrace Law #2, pause and reconsider before you tell anyone about a problem you are experiencing. Think about whether your problem will keep someone's world from turning. If it will, ask yourself the following questions:

- Is there another approach I can take to get this job done?
- If I delay for a short time, might other options appear?
- Is this *really* a problem which I cannot handle by myself?
- Is this *really* a problem at all?

If you determine that you must escalate a problem to management's attention, you must frame the problem in a way that shows you provided the necessary effort required by Law #2. For example, instead of saying: "I can't do this," consider saying: "I made progress on what you asked me to do but I hit this roadblock which I can't seem to get around. Can you help me with this part of your request?"

Focus on keeping people's worlds turning. This will show others that you are a can-do person. They will look to you as someone they can trust to make things happen. They will come to you when they need to be sure that something gets done. When you enable someone's world to keep turning peacefully, the size of your box will grow.

The Laws of Invisibility – Law #3

Law #3: Self-Righteousness is the enemy of Invisibility. There is a difference between doing the right thing and getting the right thing done. Do what works, not what you believe is right just because it is right.

Assess was about recognizing Self-Righteousness and understanding its destructive impact on you and what you *really* want. "The *Right* Thing" can be relative. Review the definition of Self-Righteousness:

Self-Righteous – *adjective* – Convinced of one's own righteousness especially in contrast with the actions and beliefs of others: narrow-mindedly moralistic.

Is it more important to you to be *right* in a situation, when being right may prevent a greater good from happening or when it may prevent you from getting what you *really* want?

Example: *AirSPACE*

Law #3: Get the Right Thing Done

Andrew
Supervisor

|

Bryant
Engineer

AirSPACE is not very good about recognizing its employees through rewards and recognition. That is why, when Bryant was told he was being nominated for the Project Management Excellence (PME) award, he was very excited. Only five PME awards are given out each year within AirSPACE and it was prestigious to be on the nomination list. As an added bonus, the team leader for any project that wins the award receives a $200 bonus.

Andrew sent Bryant the eight-page PME award nomination form via e-mail and asked him to fill it out. Bryant was disappointed that Andrew did not make the effort to fill out the form himself but he was still excited about the prospect of receiving the award. So Bryant filled out the nomination forms with the required information and emailed the file back to Andrew.

Andrew met with Bryant a few days later. Andrew began: "Bryant, I reviewed the form and I had a number of changes." Andrew handed a printout of the form to Bryant covered with corrections made in red pen. Bryant quickly reviewed the changes and noted that Andrew had crossed out some team members and added some different ones. When he asked about those changes, Andrew told him: "You listed some suppliers as team members. Suppliers are not eligible for the award. In addition, there are some other people I wanted listed as team members."

Bryant immediately felt frustrated. First, he felt annoyed that Andrew would mark up the nomination form instead of entering the changes himself. Andrew's lack of effort to reward him did not feel to Bryant like "recognition." Bryant felt that this nomination, which was supposed to be an award, was turning out to be a lot of busy work. More importantly, Bryant was upset about the changes to the team membership. The suppliers he had listed were instrumental to the project's success. Without their hard work, they would have never finished on time and within budget. In addition, the people Andrew added were some of Andrew's friends who had nothing to do with the project. Bryant could not believe that he was unable to acknowledge the people who worked so hard on the project and was being forced to falsely recognize others. Bryant recognized this as a moment when he needed some serious ball centering. He took the papers, thanked Andrew, and thought of a reason to get up and walk away. Excusing himself, he took a long walk to cool off. He resolved not to think about this until tomorrow.

The next day, Bryant considered his options. Would he tell Andrew he was not going to change the team list? Would he turn down the nomination? Would he just make the changes that Andrew told him to make? Was there another option here that he was not currently considering? He decided to go back to Assess…what did he *really* want from this situation?

He listed his goals:

- Don't get a smaller box
- Get a bigger box

- Get a nomination
- Get an award (if possible)
- Recognize and thank the people who were responsible for the project's success

The first thing he recognized was that all of his goals were very SPACEable. None of these *Really* Wants contained underlying Self-Righteousness. The second thing he recognized was that AirSPACE, in its own way, was making an effort to recognize him. The last thing he wanted to do was turn this potentially positive situation into a situation that left him with a smaller box.

If Bryant told Andrew he would not change the team members, he would create Heat. He looked at his list of goals and realized that this course of action would not achieve a single one. Likewise, if he simply turned down the nomination, he would not achieve any of the goals listed. But what would happen if he cheerfully made the changes? Which of the five goals would he achieve?

First, Bryant would get a bigger box. Andrew wants Bryant to make the changes. Making the changes would increase Andrew's confidence that Bryant is an employee who will give him what he *really* wants. Bryant would not be creating Heat, so he would not get a smaller box. If he made the changes, he would certainly get the nomination. Getting the nomination would make it possible for him to achieve the award (which would look great on his performance review). So far, so good: Bryant would get four out of five goals met with this course of action. What about thanking the people for the project's success? How could he get his team recognized, especially his suppliers (who were not even eligible to receive the award)?

Bryant determined that with the bonus, he would treat the suppliers to a thank-you lunch. He would buy a nice card with a personal note of thanks for each supplier. He would explain that the rules of the award preclude suppliers from receiving it but he hopes this thank-you lunch will show his appreciation on behalf of AirSPACE.

There are other side-benefits from receiving the PME nomination. This nomination would go on the record for the local facility; it would look good for the local management if Bryant was actually awarded the PME.

What would Bryant give up by getting his five goals met? Well, he would need to change the names just as Andrew asked. Bryant is not happy with this course of action. However, he understands Organizational Mechanics…and this is part of his Invisibility Pain. It is a disappointing fact of life in a High-Friction Organization. This course of action would give AirSPACE and his local management what they *really* want. Furthermore, it would give Bryant what he *really* wants. Andrew gets his choice of names added so he would get what he *really* wants. It would even be good for the suppliers because, instead of getting nothing, they would get a nice thank-you lunch. Is it better to be Self-Righteous about the team list, preventing everyone from getting what they *really* want? Or is it better to get the right thing done so everyone gets what they *really* want? Bryant's choice to agree to Andrew's changes was a win-win-win decision.

Consider some points about Friction, Heat, and integrity. First, remember that Friction is the organization's problem and Heat is the individual's problem. The Friction in the PME example is a characteristic of AirSPACE. Bryant cannot do anything to change that Friction; resisting it will only create Heat and give Bryant a smaller box. However, Heat is clearly Bryant's choice. Bryant can be Self-Righteous, say "This is wrong!" and ultimately create Heat. All this will do is give Bryant a smaller box. Friction is the organization's problem and Heat is the individual's problem.

Consider, also, the concept of integrity in this situation. Does Andrew have an integrity problem? He may – it is not moral to use a situation to give credit to people who were not involved with a project. It is not truthful to inappropriately reward friends through the use of a company program.

Does Bryant have an integrity problem by agreeing to the request? He supposed that those people may have helped on the project in ways he was not aware. Andrew asked Bryant to put names on the team list. Bryant is complying with an order from his supervisor; he is not lying by creating this team list.

You may say: "This is a slippery slope. Just because you are complying with orders doesn't make it right." There are shades of gray in this situation. The presence of Friction means that things will not be perfect or ideal. SPACE requires you to accept the realities of Organizational Mechanics. Sometimes you must accept certain situations in the short term, such as adding names of people who did not participate on a team to a team list. Ultimately, with your bigger box, you will be more accepted by your organization, which can lead to more personal and position power. Work to increase the size of your box. Then, when you are in the position to give an award to your employees, make the choice not to ask your employee to falsely add names to the team list. Choose to fill out the nomination form yourself, just as you wanted your supervisor to do.

In Assess, you determined your Bottom Lines. Your Bottom Lines enable you to maintain your integrity in gray situations. Make sure you understand them and how they apply in various situations. If your Bottom Lines are that you will not compromise safety, then adding a few names to a team list does not violate them. More importantly, it ensures that everyone in the situation gets what they *really* want.

In the Presence of Friction, Center Your Ball and Get the Right Thing Done

High-Friction Organizations will give you plenty of opportunities to create Heat. Friction means there are people within the organization who are more focused on something other than the organization's stated goals. This can make working in a High-Friction Organization very tricky. Assess showed you the evils of Self-Righteousness. When you can list your *Really* Wants, you must maintain focus on acting in ways that help you achieve them. If your *Really* Wants are honorable, accept the Organizational Mechanics of the situation which says that there will be some Invisibility Pain involved in life within your organization. Acting Invisibly will surely increase the size of your box, enabling you to do things you think are important. Self-Righteousness is the enemy that is always ready to keep you from getting what you *really* want.

The Laws of Invisibility – Law #4

> **Law #4:** Don't give people what they want; give them what they *really* want. Anticipate people's needs so you can give them what they *really* want.

SPACE is about getting what you *really* want. However, everyone else in your organization also wants to get what they *really* want. To get what you *really* want, you must give others what they *really* want. You must do more than listen to what people ask for. You must observe their behavior to get clues about their true intentions. You must get to know them and their motivations so you can match their words and their actions. Only then can you give someone what they *really* want.

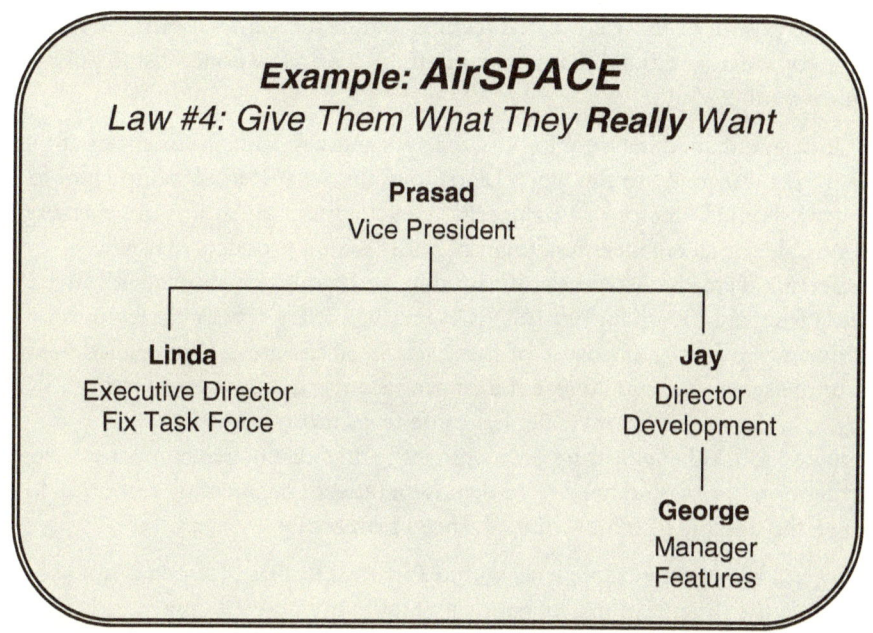

Example: *AirSPACE*
*Law #4: Give Them What They **Really** Want*

Prasad
Vice President

Linda
Executive Director
Fix Task Force

Jay
Director
Development

George
Manager
Features

SPACE is not just for people at lower levels within organizations. Those who are at the highest levels of High-Friction Organizations are natural SPACE Creators. They must be, in order to reach their position. An executive director named Linda was recently in a situation where she effectively avoided creating Heat while giving everyone what they *really* wanted.

Linda was appointed to lead a Fix Task Force for seating features. Many in the executive jet industry had been adding design features to cabin seats to make them more comfortable and useful to passengers. AirSPACE, in recent years, had added video screens, heated cushions, lumbar support, and built-in neck support into their seats. Unfortunately, those functions did not always work and AirSPACE received complaints from their customers that the advanced seat features were unreliable. The need to resolve the problems with the seat features had been elevated to the highest levels at AirSPACE. Linda, a very shrewd and capable executive director, was appointed to lead the team that would ensure the problems with the seating features were fixed.

Linda and her team gave regular progress reports to Prasad, an AirSPACE vice-president. They reported to Prasad every month, and, over time, Prasad grew tired of hearing about the never-ending problems with the seating features. Finally, in one progress report, he lost his temper. He said: "I am *so* tired of the continuing problems with all these seating features. I can't understand why you all continue to be unable to fix these problems!" Then he pointed to Linda and continued: "Linda, I want you to go to Jay and tell him I'm done. I want you to tell Jay to pull all of these advanced features out of the seats. I want the seat *so* simple to design and build that you won't mess it up. I'm done. I want all the features out!!"

Linda maintained her cool to outward appearances. But she knew what this meant. Jay was going to flip when Linda told him what Prasad wanted him to do. Jay was the Director of Engineering Development at AirSPACE. Jay was responsible for all engineering design of AirSPACE's products. Jay's engineering teams had spent significant time and money developing advanced seating features. In addition, AirSPACE received a large premium from their customers for the seats because of these advanced features. If Jay pulled them out of the seats, they would lose the enormous investment in engineering resources, the additional revenue that came from those features (which continued to fund engineering development), and a distinctive competitive edge. Furthermore, Jay would need to re-deploy significant engineering resources to change the designs to remove the advanced features.

Jay and Linda are at same level within AirSPACE; that is, Linda is not above Jay within the organization's hierarchy and Jay is not above Linda. Linda knew that, even though she did not make the request to have the features removed, Jay would resent Linda for this situation. After all, Linda was on the Fix Task Force and the apparent action from the task force was to have all of the features removed. Why couldn't Prasad have told Jay himself, Linda thought? Prasad had put her in a bad position by making this demand – Jay could now blame Linda for the decision even though *Prasad* made the decision. Prasad had made the demand in front of a large team of people, removing the option of negotiating with Prasad about his position. Prasad was known to be stubborn, especially when he made decrees in front of large groups of people.

As with most skilled SPACE Creators, Linda took time to ensure that her ball was centered. Then she went back to SPACE basics. What was it that Prasad *really* wanted? Did he *really* want the advanced seating features removed? No, he did not. He knew those features generated a huge amount of revenue. He knew there would be a lot of effort required to take the features out. He knew it would cost the company competitive edge and reputation. Linda knew from SPACE that, in High-Friction Organizations, people do not say what they *really* want. So what did he *really* want?

Linda knew that Prasad just wanted the problems to go away. He saw, month after month, that the problems were not being addressed effectively. He had little faith in the people within AirSPACE to successfully fix the problems. So, like an exhausted parent with a child who continues to misbehave, he made a final and exasperated dictate. He did not want to lose the revenue, the investment, and the competitive edge, if possible. He just wanted the problems to go away.

Linda also thought about what she *really* wanted. First and foremost, she wanted to get out of this difficult situation without a smaller box. It would be an unexpected reward for her ability to create SPACE if she were actually able to expand the size of her box through this.

Linda knew she was Invisible to her coworkers, including Jay. She knew that acting Invisibly to your coworkers will increase the size of your box by building goodwill. Linda thought about what Jay *really* wanted. Well, he certainly does not want to lose the revenue from the seating features. He does not want to re-deploy his engineering resources to undo work that they had already done. She also thought of Law #2. Linda knew Jay would not graciously embrace the effort to remove the seating features. She knew that Jay just wanted his world to keep turning.

Linda came up with a new option. She decided to visit George, the manager of the advanced seating features. George works for Jay and is Jay's manager responsible for everything related to AirSPACE's seats. In addition, George is below Linda within the AirSPACE hierarchy. Linda paid him a visit the next day.

She began: "George, I was in our Fix Task Force review yesterday. We reviewed the latest information on the problems that our customers are experiencing with the advanced features. Prasad is tired of the problems and wants you to tell Jay to remove all of the features." Then she stopped talking to let the effect of the news sink in with George. The news hit George like a punch. "He can't do that – what is he, crazy?!" George recounted all of the things Linda knew – the loss of revenue and everything else. He thought about what it would be like to deliver this news to Jay. Then George got quiet. He thought about something that Linda knew…Jay was going to rake George over the coals for this. In High-Friction Organizations, blame is passed along and placed squarely on the highest person who cannot defend it. That person was George. George's department was directly responsible for the quality of the advanced seating features and he would certainly take the fall for these problems. Very quickly, he became scared of what would happen. He was, in that instant, very emotionally engaged in the situation and Linda saw the expressions on his face – she knew what he was thinking.

"All right," she said, "I'll tell you what we can do, George. Prasad said, unambiguously, that he wanted the advanced seating features removed. I don't have to report back to him next month. That gives you two months. I want you to develop a plan to run reliability tests on all of the advanced features. I want a full and thorough report on every single feature's performance. Then I want to see good, solid, and concrete plans for fixing the designs that do not meet our quality standards. I want engineering proof that you can build these features reliably. And I want those tests completed in five weeks. If you can give me rock-solid proof that these problems will go away, I will bring your data to Prasad and support the position to keep the features in the seats. If you can't give me the proof I need, *you* are going to tell Jay that he needs to develop the plans to remove the features from the seats."

Give 'em What They *Really* Want

The above example shows excellent application of the first three Laws of Invisibility. First, Linda did not resist Prasad's request, as ludicrous as it was. She used conciliation and left the immediate situation. In doing so, she bought time to develop a win-win solution. Second, she thought about whose world needed to keep turning. She knew that she could work effectively through the people in Jay's department without alerting Jay to a problem that may never come to pass. In fact, Jay may only learn of this after the problem is solved effectively, without his intervention. Third, Linda did not let her Self-Righteousness ball get knocked off center. She knew she had been given a direct order...shouldn't people do what they are told? However, she knew that the right thing for AirSPACE was to fix the problem. Removing the features would be equivalent to cutting off one's nose to spite one's face. Even though she was disobeying a direct order from a senior executive, she was taking a calculated risk to create a situation where everyone benefits.

Most importantly, she understood that she needed to give people what they *really* wanted. She astutely evaluated the situation and gave people the following *Really* Wants:

Prasad: The problems with the advanced seating features *will* go away. Either the features will be fixed or they will be removed.

Jay: His world will keep turning. His team will fully get the chance to fix the problem before losing the revenue and investment. Even better, his team will be working with a high sense of urgency without any intervention on his part.

George: He will get a full and fair chance to fix a problem for which he is responsible without added pressure from Jay.

To be an effective SPACE Creator, you must not get *overly* caught-up by what people say. In High-Friction Organizations, what people *say* they want is frequently different than what they *really* want. You must listen carefully to people; you cannot continually and blatantly ignore direct requests. However, when you look on a deeper level and truly understand what people around you *really* want, you may find the opportunity to take a calculated risk to deliver something great. Linda's solution was exceptional and elegant. She did not get herself into trouble even though she was placed in a difficult situation. She created a solution that made everyone very happy.

In summary, Linda started by looking after herself. She bought time in spite of an emotionally charged situation and ensured that her ball was centered. She ascertained people's true intentions and desires and did not allow her hands to be tied by what people *said* they wanted. She worked with subordinates in other departments so her colleague's world would keep turning. Note that George will be very appreciative of Linda's approach – he will see this as a favor that he will be more than willing to repay at some time in the future. Finally, she did much more than the damage control of avoiding a smaller box. She increased the size of her box and created a solution where *everybody* won.

The Laws of Invisibility – Law #5

Law #5: Accept that Invisibility comes with a Low Level of Pain. Some energy will be wasted as Heat and Non-Useful Work.

Law #5 is a reminder of the Law of Conservation of Organizational Energy. Nothing is free in life, and living Invisibly has its cost. The cost is enduring the low level of Invisibility Pain which you feel working in your High Friction Organization.

The Low Level of Pain comes from accepting the fact that things within your organization are simply not going to be as good as you want them to be. Friction prevents 'the right thing' from getting done. It is simply the physics of the situation which you cannot change.

The Low Level of Pain comes from doing Non-Useful Work which you know will not help your organization reach its stated goals. You feel pain because Friction requires you to work *harder* but not *smarter*. The Low Level of Pain comes from doing things you know are not in the best interests of the Company or their Stakeholders. It comes from acting in ways which you would never act in a Low-Friction Organization. It is the pain you feel today in exchange for the increased maneuvering room that will help you do bigger and better things tomorrow. It is the pain you feel from walking away from a good battle, so you can ultimately win the war.

The Low Level of Pain is also from accepting the impropriety of Invisibility. It is not right that people can ignore you and your talents and gifts. It is not right that people who are higher than you in the organization's hierarchy can choose to ignore you. It is painful to accept that refusing to act Invisibly will only relegate you to failure and frustration in your organization.

The Low Level of Pain is actually the energy you release when you Center Your Ball. Ball centering is not a passive endeavor; it requires focus and control, which requires energy. It makes you tired and saps energy you would rather use for the good of the organization. It is also represented in the Goals-Righteousness Model by the spring tension between your true goals and your organization's true goals. When you are in a High-Friction Organization, there will always be a constant, nagging tension trying to pull you away from making great things happen.

A final and important note about the Low Level of Pain: The Low Level of Pain beats the pain you will feel from creating Heat – any time, and any day.

> **The Low Level of Pain beats the pain you will feel from creating Heat – any time, any day!!**

Your freedom and ability to make extraordinary things happen in a High-Friction Organization is dependent on the size of your box. If you create Heat, your box will shrink. With a smaller box, you are less able to make the changes you want to make. When you choose to accept a situation that activates your Self-Righteousness, you will feel a measure of pain. By accepting that situation, you will maintain or increase the size of your box, enabling you to fight a more effective fight at a later date. Remember: Invisibility ultimately results in win-win for you and your High-Friction Organization. When you create Heat, nobody gets what they really want; everyone loses.

The Laws of Invisibility – Law #6

> **Law #6:** Do not engage difficult people.

You must always be careful around Point Sources of Friction (or difficult people). Difficult people are full of negative energy and are ready and willing to help you create Heat. To ensure that you avoid shrinking your box, take care never to engage a difficult person.

Example: *AirSPACE*

Law #6: Do Not Engage Difficult People

Nancy
Supervisor
|
Philip   **Brad**
Engineer   Engineer

Philip worked at the Engine Teardown facility at AirSPACE. Engines were brought to the facility after they were used in jets. Engineers would disassemble the engines to review the components and understand how well they had performed.

Brad was an engineer on a review team that regularly visited the teardown facility. From the beginning, Brad proved himself to be difficult. He never cleaned up the area before he left. He treated others with disrespect and had an air of indifference that left anyone who interacted with him feeling frustrated.

One week, when Brad's team was at the facility, they were looking at heavy engine parts. When Brad finished inspecting a part, he would throw it with great force into a dumpster. The sound shot through the large facility and startled people who were standing a good distance away. Brad would smirk when he saw people jump.

After ten minutes of this behavior, Philip's supervisor Nancy came to the teardown area and asked Brad to kindly place his parts gently into the dumpster. Brad looked at Nancy, took the next heavy part, and threw it with great force into the dumpster. Nancy left the room and brought the facility manager to the area. Right when the facility manager walked in, Brad found a particularly heavy part to throw into the dumpster. People in the room rubbed their heads from the noise. The facility manager reaffirmed Nancy's request to stop being so disruptive. Brad shrugged his shoulders and tossed another part loudly into the dumpster. The inspection ended shortly thereafter.

Two weeks later, Brad's team was back at the facility. This time, they were measuring ball bearings from the engine. Brad was using expensive measurement equipment called micrometers to take measurements on the ball bearings. He needed to open a cardboard box that contained additional engine parts, so he used part of these micrometers as a razor blade to open the box.

Everyone in AirSPACE knew that micrometers were sensitive measurement equipment. Using them as a tool to open cardboard boxes threw them out of calibration. Philip said to Brad in an annoyed tone of voice: "Brad, you need to stop using those micrometers to open your boxes." Brad smiled and said: "Well, if I don't have a razor blade, I'm going to keep using these." He used them to open another box. Now Philip was not a SPACE creator. He quickly considered the local history with Brad. It was only a couple weeks ago that Brad challenged the facility's management. Surely Philip would receive support if he made an aggressive effort to prevent damaging the facility's expensive equipment. Philip said: "Brad, if you continue to do this, I'm going to have you removed from the facility and barred so that you never come back!"

From this point, things just got worse. Nancy became involved, there was some shouting and frustration, and Brad walked out of the facility. The facility manager was notified about the situation and Nancy met with some witnesses to better understand what had happened.

An hour later, Philip was sitting in Nancy's office discussing the situation. Philip said: "Working with Brad has been *so* frustrating. But I was surprised to see him treat our equipment like he did." Nancy listened, then said: "Look Philip, you need to try to be a little more accommodating with the people who use our facility. I talked with the facility manager and we think we may need to move you to another area since there are personality problems now."

Philip was dumbfounded. He said to himself: "Personality problems? Brad is the same guy who was so belligerent and disrespectful to everyone here just a couple weeks before. Now you are suggesting that I have a personality problem here??!?" Speechless, Philip just listened to Nancy talk for a while. When she was done, he stood up and left her office, trying to figure out what just happened.

Never Wrestle with a Pig

Have you heard the expression: "Never wrestle with a pig. You both get dirty and the pig likes it."? This expression holds significant truth, especially in High-Friction Organizations. When you engage a difficult person in a High-Friction Organization, you should expect yourself to become labeled as a difficult person.

In the above example, everyone knew Brad was difficult. Brad's own management must have known he was difficult. Philip's management *throughout the facility* knew Brad was difficult. But the fact that Brad still worked at AirSPACE reveals a very important decision: AirSPACE has made a *conscious decision* not to address Brad and the problems he causes. This key fact reveals why Philip was punished for his approach to the situation. If everyone clearly wanted to ignore the problem, what made Philip think *he* could fix it? Philip was trying to fix a problem *that his management consciously decided they didn't want to fix.* He had even involved one of the exact managers who had chosen to ignore the problem!

Consider Probe's implications for this example. Brad, like all difficult people, is a *Point Source* of Friction. When you engage them inappropriately, you rub against Friction and create Heat. Like any other Source of Friction, Brad can serve a useful purpose for someone higher in the organization. Difficult people can be used as a diversion within High Friction Organizations because of their natural tendency to create Heat wherever they go. Maybe Brad's management uses him in situations where they want to distract others away from another problem. Keeping a counterproductive and disruptive employee in a job cannot help an organization achieve its stated goals. The fact that Brad still works within the organization indicates that someone wants to keep him there or does not want to deal with removing him.

This example also shows how Law #6 supports previous Laws of Invisibility. In this example, Philip broke every single previous Law!

- He broke Law #1 by not being conciliatory with Brad. As a result, he did not create SPACE...he lost SPACE. Ultimately, he achieved nothing important through his actions.

- Philip broke Law #2 because his management would have rather that their worlds just kept turning. Instead, Philip brought a problem to them when the problem could easily have been avoided entirely.

- Self-Righteousness was the enemy of Philip's Invisibility. Because he was so focused on being right, his approach to fix Brad's bad behavior resulted only in negative effects for himself. If Philip had just centered his ball and found a razor blade for Brad, Philip would have gotten what he *really* wanted without shrinking his own box.

- Philip did not follow Law #4 because he did not observe the organization's behavior to understand what it *really* wanted. The organization, through its previous actions, clearly demonstrated that it did not want to deal with the problems Brad caused. If Philip had recognized this, he never would have acted the way he did.

- Philip did not accept the Low Level of Pain described in Law #5. Instead of accepting this lingering problem week after week, he tried to 'do the right thing' and eliminate the problem. Even though Brad was causing a lot of Non-Useful Work, this Low Level of Pain was certainly better for Philip to accept than creating Heat by attempting to eliminate the problem. After all that had happened, the problem (Brad) was *still* not addressed, but now Philip was viewed as a liability and had a smaller box from the incident.

- Finally, Philip broke Law #6 when he engaged Brad, who had proven to be a very difficult person.

The Laws of Invisibility – Law #7

> **Law #7:** You will not get the credit you want. You must accept the credit you get.

In High-Friction Organizations, 'do-the-right-thing' people will often feel unrewarded for their efforts. As you learned in Probe, what an individual believes is 'the right thing' is different from what the High-Friction Organization believes is 'the right thing.' If the organization believes that an individual is not giving it what it *really* wants, it will not reward that individual. This also explains why others are rewarded when you do not believe they 'do-the-right-thing': they give the organization what it *really* wants.

The expectation of 'credit' for 'good work' is dangerous because it affects your Self-Righteousness. If you believe you should be rewarded for working long hours or for extra efforts, you will be disappointed when you do not receive those rewards. You will think: "This isn't right!" Your Self-Righteousness ball will start to rise. You may even act out of this Self-Righteousness against others in your organization. Of course, this will only shrink your box and further increase your frustration.

To ensure that you live Invisibly and continuously increase the size of your box, you must not expect "credit." You must focus on what you learned from Assess about what you *really* want. Success through Invisibility means that you are satisfied when you get what you *really* want. Special commendations will not happen for things your organization does not value, regardless of how important you believe they are. You must accept this Low Level of Pain from not being appreciated for your good work so you can keep your ball centered.

Credit can come from unlikely places. Recall the example used to illustrate Law #1. Allison never received 'due credit' from Marcus for creating and implementing an effective inventory management program. The unexpected credit she received for doing her good work was the going-away party and presents that her coworkers gave her when she left AirSPACE. If you continuously work to give people around you what they *really* want, rewards will ultimately find their way back to you.

The Laws of Invisibility – Law #8

> **Law #8:** Always remember your place as an Invisible person. Deference is necessary when you are Invisible. Bumping back is seldom successful.

Living Invisibly is a lifestyle that accepts a constant dull ache: the Low Level of Pain. It is the price you pay for making the best of a situation that is not ideal. It is easier to accept when you are aware that you are getting what you *really* want. Yet even if you are getting what you *really* want, accepting the reality of your Invisibility is difficult over time. Sometimes, you will want to shout about it. You will want to scream to the world: "I am *not* Invisible!!!" You will want to act out against the people who are reinforcing this demeaning structure of Invisibility. Law # 8 is a reminder that you must always remember your place as an Invisible person. Sometimes you may feel like you want to bump back against the people around you so you can *feel* like you are really not Invisible. Bumping back seldom does anything but create Heat.

Example: *AirSPACE*

Law #8: Bumping Back is Seldom Successful

Dave
Supervisor
|
Bryant
Engineer

Bryant had called a meeting in a conference room in his building. His meeting included two engineering colleagues, a supplier, and two production workers. At the start of the meeting, they spread out their papers and made notes on the white-board in the room. They had been meeting and working for ten minutes when Dave walked into the room with two other people. Dave is the Supervisor who was identified as a Point Source of Friction. Dave is focused on position power and, therefore, *really* wants people to show him respect and deference.

Dave looked at everyone working in the room, then said to Bryant: "I need this conference room." Bryant thought for a minute. He had scheduled the conference room for his working meeting and had even verified that the room was not otherwise reserved. Bryant knew there were three other conference rooms down the hall. He could even see one of those rooms and noticed it was vacant. Finally, Bryant knew that Dave did this often: Dave would not check conference room schedules prior to holding meetings. Dave would just assume that he could come in and take the room if the people occupying the room were beneath him in the organization.

So what should Bryant do?

Bryant is a SPACE creator and knows what Dave *really* wants. His Self-Righteousness ball was elevated because he felt demeaned by Dave. However, he knows that asking Dave to take the vacant conference room was nothing more than challenging Dave's position power. Resisting him will only create Heat. Dave's actions are supported by the Ambient Source of the organization's negative attitude towards subordinates. Bumping back against Dave and his inappropriate treatment, especially in front of an audience, would simply give Bryant a smaller box.

Bryant looked around at the papers they would have to move to the other conference room. He looked up at the whiteboard and saw that they would need to copy a page of notes and transfer it to the board in the other room. He wanted to shout: "Why don't you use some common courtesy and schedule your own conference room??! Why don't you open your eyes and look across the hall to see that there's an empty room only ten steps away??!" But, instead, Bryant inhaled slowly, centered his ball, looked up at Dave, smiled and said: "Sure, Dave; no problem. There's an open conference room right across the hall. We'll copy our notes off the white-board and we'll be out of here immediately."

What did Bryant lose from this? He incurred about five minutes of Non-Useful Work and lost some energy which he used to center his ball. Perhaps he gained some goodwill with Dave. The next time Bryant asks something from Dave, Dave may be more inclined to help him. Dave certainly would not be so inclined if Bryant had challenged him. Bryant likely increased the size of his box by following Law #8. More importantly, Bryant certainly did not shrink his box from the encounter.

Invisibility – Management Implications

Invisibility does not set up an environment where employees will be motivated to give their best effort. Managers may wonder how they can manage within a High-Friction Organization in a way that *does* get the best from their employees. Fortunately, this is entirely within a manager's control in a High-Friction Organization. *Managers in High-Friction Organizations set the Invisibility Structure for the people below them in the organization.* That is, managers determine the degree to which they will accept the behaviors of Invisibility in their organization.

An Invisible person only creates Heat when they do not give someone what they *really* want. If you are a manager who *wants* your employees to push back and challenge your ideas, you will not perceive these challenges as Heat. Therefore, you must communicate your expectations to your employees. However, what you *say* to set the Invisibility structure is much less important than what you actually *do*.

Effective SPACE Creators in High-Friction Organizations are constantly observing people's behaviors to understand what they *really* want. If SPACE Creators see one of your employees provide an alternative for a project which is different from the direction you have given, they will watch your reaction. If you react with punishment and degradation, they will assume that you do not *really* want opposing points of view, regardless of what you say. If SPACE Creators determine that you want people to just do what you say, they will act accordingly.

Managing with a Low-Friction style in a High-Friction Organization requires an unusual amount of communication, trust, and consistent behavior. Employees who have performed a good Survey will recognize Friction in the organization and will accept their Invisibility. Further, their Invisibility will be reinforced by their treatment from others. If you wish to make a different work environment for your employees, you must work harder to build their trust. You must constantly communicate your expectations for a different way of operation and back up your words with concrete actions. You must seek out and actively reward people for doing the right thing, regardless of how that is valued by the organization.

Managing in this way carries some perils. If your employees recognize that they are less Invisible to you, they may assume they are less Invisible to other managers within the organization. This may make them more apt to create Heat when interfacing with others. In High-Friction Organizations, when your employees create Heat, that Heat may find its way back to you. You may be answerable for your employees' actions. In this situation, you must find a way to help your employees understand that what is not Heat for you may be Heat for someone else. If your employees create Heat outside of your organization, that Heat can shrink your own box. When your own box gets smaller, you will have less opportunity to make the positive impact you wish to make. You must use caution when managing without Invisibility in a High-Friction Organization.

Create Space - Conclusions

Your success in your organization is greatly impacted by your interface. That is, your success is largely determined by your *behaviors*. Sometimes, success in a High-Friction Organization has less to do with *results* and more to do with *behaviors*. The Laws of Invisibility prescribe the behaviors that any organization, especially a High-Friction Organization, will value.

If you understand Invisibility, you will be able to effectively evaluate a situation to understand its capacity to create Heat. If you live according to the Laws of Invisibility, you will work in a way that does not create Heat. More of your energy and the energy of those around you will be converted into Useful Work. Your organization will appreciate the *way* you deliver your great work and will reward you with a bigger box.

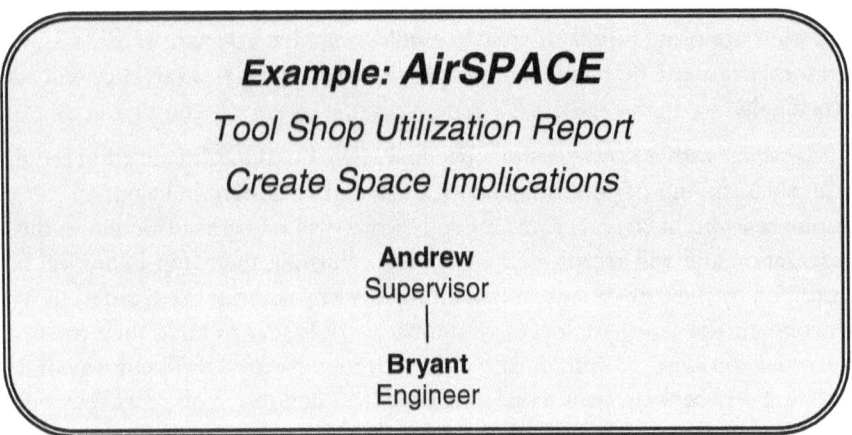

Bryant has a good understanding of what Andrew *really* wants. Bryant knows his own *Really* Wants. He considers each of the Laws of Invisibility and how they would guide him in this situation:

- Law #1 tells Bryant to use conciliation and detachment. Both are applicable here: conciliation and detachment tell Bryant to detach, smile, and say: "I can do that, Andrew."

- Law #2 tells Bryant not to be difficult with Andrew. Andrew would rather his world kept turning and that he got the report with the big numbers he wanted.

- Law #3 tells Bryant not to become Self-Righteous about what he believes is the right thing to do. Ultimately, he needs to get the right thing done.

- Law #4 tells Bryant that, at this moment, Andrew *really* wants a report which keeps senior management away from their facility.

- Law #5 tells Bryant that agreeing with Andrew's request is really just a part of the Low Level of Pain of working in a High-Friction Organization. The Low Level of Pain beats the pain Bryant would feel from creating Heat.

- Law #6 tells Bryant that Andrew could be considered a difficult person in this situation and there is no reason to engage him.

- Law #7 tells Bryant that he simply will not get the credit for creating a great report no matter how much he resists Andrew.

- Law #8 tells Bryant that creating Heat with Andrew to feel better about this situation will ultimately give Bryant a smaller box.

It was clear to Bryant how the Laws of Invisibility guide him in this situation.

Key Points from Create Space:

1) You are Invisible to someone if they can choose to ignore you and not suffer any negative personal consequences in the organization.

2) You create Heat if you are Invisible to someone but you act as if you are **V**isible.

3) The Laws of Invisibility provide a solid toolkit for helping you tune your interface with your organization.

4) The Laws of Invisibility are especially useful in High-Friction Organizations. Since they are focused on giving people what they *really* want, they are effective in any organization and any situation in which you must work with others.

Now that you know what your organization *really* wants and what you *really* want, live according to the Laws of Invisibility. You will maximize your impact, feel less frustrated, and be rewarded by your organization.

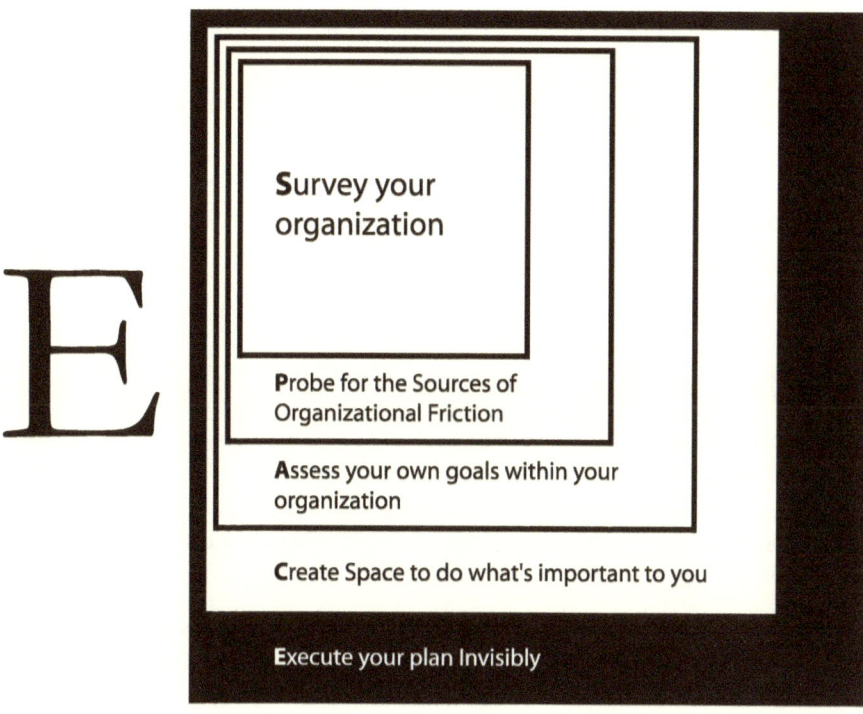

E

Creating SPACE is not natural; if it were, everyone would already be doing it. Like any habit you establish, you will need constant reminders of the new interface you are trying to create with your organization.

Execute contains tools and concepts to help you successfully learn and apply SPACE until it becomes second nature. These tools and concepts will keep SPACE in your mind when you are in the presence of Friction. SPACE will ease the frustration caused by seemingly irrational and confusing events so you do not create Heat. Execute will help you stay centered and ensure that everyone in a situation – including you – is getting what they *really* want.

> The tools and concepts in Execute will help you continue to expand your box...and will keep you from shrinking your box.

Execute will ensure that you work Invisibly to get what you *really* want.

The tools and concepts that the Execute chapter will demonstrate are:

- Invisibility Law #8…a and b
- Low Level of Pain Coping Strategies
- The Credit Trap
- SPACE Loops
- SPACE Partners
- The Rate of SPACE Creation/Box Expansion
- SPACE Maps

Invisibility Law #8…a and b

The first seven Laws of Invisibility are constant regardless of the size of your box. "Give people what they *really* want" or "Do not engage difficult people" mean the same thing whether your box is large or small. However, Law #8 is unique; it means something subtly different depending on the size of your box. Recall Law #8:

> Always remember your place as an Invisible person.
> Deference is necessary when you are Invisible. Bumping
> back is seldom successful.

When your box is small, this law takes on a slightly different meaning than if your box is large. These differences are defined to be Law #8a and Law #8b:

Law #8a (for someone with a small box): Bumping back is seldom successful.

Law #8b (for someone with a large box): Always remember that you are still Invisible.

Law #8a

When you have a small box, it is easy to become frustrated. You are constantly aware of your Invisibility and feel as if you are less significant. You may not receive much positive feedback and affirmation from your organization. It is natural to feel resentful and angry about this treatment. You may even feel like bumping back and lashing out at someone who makes you feel Invisible.

Bumping back is seldom successful.

You know that an Invisible lifestyle carries with it a Low Level of Pain. It takes time to expand your box because those around you have a preconceived notion that you will continue to create Heat. It takes time to convince others that something has changed. As you continue to create SPACE, you may feel impatient. Your Low Level of Pain increases because you are accepting the Non-Useful Work that is part of working in a High-Friction Organization. You work hard to check your emotions so you can stop creating Heat. Over time, your frustration builds and you will want (or need) a break from the control which you have been so careful to exercise. Creating just a small amount of Heat will be a setback for the effort you have invested in expanding your box. As your box grows, always remember your place as an Invisible person.

Choosing to live Invisibly and accept the frustrations associated with Friction means you expend energy to keep your ball centered. That energy flow is the Low Level of Pain. You choose whether you convert your Organizational Energy into Invisibility Pain or into Heat. When you live Invisibly, you will continue to create SPACE and increase the size of your box. The alternative is to give in to your frustration and negative emotion and use your energy to create Heat.

Therefore, Law #8a reminds you that bumping back is seldom successful. This desire to bump back and create Heat – even a small amount of Heat – must be actively managed. To manage this impulse, you must first recognize and accept that the Low Level of Pain is difficult to live with. It is not natural for you to accept that things are not as efficient or as effective as they could be. It is painful to look Point Sources of Friction in the eye, smile and say: "I can do that." You must recognize that living Invisibly is challenging. Do not minimize the pain of it; minimizing the significance of the Low Level of Pain will make it unbearable.

To ensure that you keep your ball centered and do not bump back, use Low Level of Pain Coping Strategies. Low Level of Pain Coping Strategies ensure that you continue to channel your energy into Centering Your Ball and not into Heat.

Three Low Level of Pain Coping Strategies are:

- Keeping your eyes on the prize
- Organizational Mechanics reminders
- SPACE partners

Keep your Eye on the Prize

The first Low Level of Pain Coping Strategy is to "keep your eye on the prize." You are living an Invisible lifestyle so you can get what you *really* want. You must constantly remind yourself of your *Really* Wants so, as you work within your High-Friction Organization, you will remember why you are exerting so much energy to keep your ball centered.

If you are creating SPACE for a promotion, write reminders of that goal in places where you will often see them. Write the word "Promotion" in your planner on a page you see every time you open it. Make it the message which appears on your PDA when you turn it on. Buy a gold pen, tell yourself it represents your promotion, and make this the pen you always use. When you use it, it will remind you why you are working so hard to Center Your Ball and give people what they *really* want.

If you are creating SPACE so you can spend more time with your family, put pictures of your family around your desk. Leave a picture of your family in your car so when you pull your key out of the ignition to go into work, you will see another glimpse of your loved ones to remind you of what you *really* want.

Be creative about keeping your *Really* Wants in front of you, especially in places where you know you will experience Friction. If you have a weekly meeting with a difficult person, keep a reminder of your *Really* Wants in your planner or under your notes. If your boss is a Point Source of Friction and frequently comes to your desk to give you assignments, put a motivational note somewhere on your desk which you can see while your boss is talking to you.

Keeping reminders of your prizes in strategic locations will help you keep your ball centered.

Remember Organizational Mechanics

As you practice creating SPACE, you will recognize that Organizational Mechanics effectively describes what happens to the Organizational Energy around you. You must remember the implications of Organizational Mechanics when you are in the presence of Friction because you are most likely to create Heat during those times. So, just as "keeping your eye on the prize" guided you to keep reminders of your *Really* Wants in strategic locations, keep SPACE diagrams in strategic locations to remind you about the existence and effects of Friction.

Think of frustrating situations, relate them to Organizational Mechanics, and put the appropriate reminder near where that situation occurs. Put an Organizational Energy pie chart in the folder you take to a frustrating meeting to remind you that some of your energy will simply be wasted as Non-Useful Work. Put the nested SPACE boxes up on the wall in your cubicle to remind you that getting a bigger box is important and helps you get what you *really* want. Use a drawing of a ball centered on the Goals-Righteousness Model axis to help you remember to Center Your Ball when you are dealing with a difficult person. Organizational Mechanics helps you make sense of confusing and frustrating situations at work. Keep reminders of Organizational Mechanics in accessible locations to remind you that it's all just physics.

SPACE Partners

Later in this chapter, you will learn about SPACE partners. A SPACE partner is someone who is familiar with SPACE concepts and knows what you *really* want. An outside opinion and perspective is invaluable, especially when trying to Center Your Ball in the midst of a difficult situation. A SPACE partner can help you refocus on your *Really* Wants so you do not bump back. Plus, it is useful to have someone who will listen and empathize in the midst of a High-Friction situation.

Law #8b and the Credit Trap

Through time, your box will grow. As you continue to create SPACE, your organization will view you as an asset because you know how to give it what it *really* wants. As your box expands and you generate more maneuvering room and space, you will *feel* your new freedom. It will feel good...*very* good. You will begin to receive credit for your efforts that you did not receive before. You will feel like your organization is recognizing your talents and rewarding you. With this increased freedom, you may believe you can now achieve more ambitious goals with greater ease. You can, but only to an extent. Because of the credit you receive, you may believe you have become less Invisible. You must remember Law #8b: Always remember that you are still Invisible. Beware not to fall into The Credit Trap.

The Credit Trap is the intoxicating feeling that credit and recognition have when you are unaccustomed to them. The Credit Trap is the belief that your organization values your accomplishments and will continue to reward you for doing things you believe are good for your organization. The Credit Trap entices you to want *more* credit and pulls you towards behaving in ways that create Heat. You *will* achieve success within your organization by creating SPACE. You may not get the credit you expected, but credit, in some form, will come your way. When it does come, you must remember Law #7: *"You will be most Invisible and create the least Heat when you work without the expectation of credit."*

High Friction Organizations do not necessarily value the same things you value. When you are rewarded for doing something great for your organization, it is more likely you are being recognized for *how* you accomplished something instead of what you actually accomplished. In High-Friction Organizations, you are more likely to be rewarded for your *behavior* instead of your *results*. The credit you receive may not be a result of what you think is valuable and important. You must continue to remember to avoid the Credit Trap so you can avoid developing unrealistic expectations of more credit.

The Credit Trap will cause you to forget the behaviors you used to increase the size of your box. If you stop thinking about Organizational Mechanics, you may forget that Friction reduces Useful Work. You may forget to live Invisibly and keep your ball centered. Your previous patterns of behavior kept your box small. It was understanding how to give people what they *really* want that made your box larger.

In summary, Law # 8, "Always remember your place as an Invisible person," takes on a different meaning when you have a larger box. Instead of reminding you not to bump back, it reminds you that you are still Invisible. Instead of encouraging you to keep your ball centered and not to bump back, it reminds you that you are still within the Invisibility structure of your organization. It reminds you to be careful not fall into the Credit Trap.

Laws #8a and #8b imply that creating SPACE is a continuous process. Creating SPACE is not something that just applies to people with small boxes. It is important for all people in High Friction Organizations to practice SPACE because *everyone* is Invisible to *someone*. SPACE concepts must be practiced constantly and consistently to transfer the maximum amount of Organizational Energy into Useful Work and the minimum amount into Heat. Because SPACE creation is continuous, SPACE Loops remind you to always strive to create SPACE in your organization.

SPACE Loops

A SPACE Loop is single cycle of the five-step SPACE process. Organizations can change due to internal events (such as promotions and reorganizations) or external events (such as changing market conditions). You must be aware of what others *really* want as changes occur. Because your *Really* Wants help you cope with Friction, they must stay relevant to help you Center Your Ball when you feel Self-Righteous. When you go through the SPACE cycle regularly, you ensure that you maintain focus on what others *really* want, and that your *Really* Wants stay current and in the forefront of your mind.

Execute

SPACE can apply to long-range goals or it can apply to an individual situation. As such, there are two types of SPACE loops: Macro SPACE Loops and Micro SPACE Loops. The diagram below shows how Macro and Micro SPACE Loops work together to ensure that you give your organization what it *really* wants and get what you *really* want.

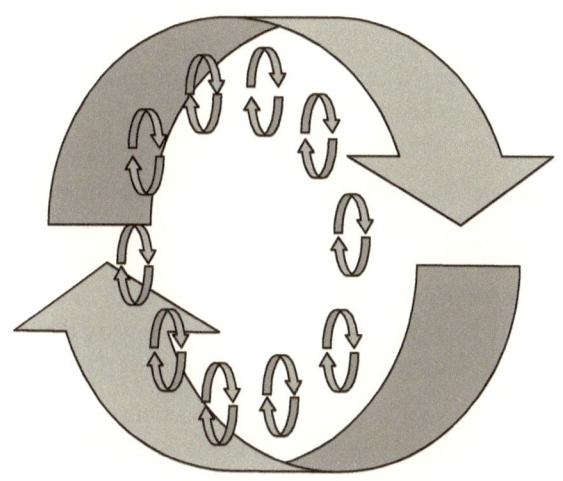

SPACE Loops

Macro SPACE Loops

The large loop encompassing the smaller loops in the above diagram represents a Macro SPACE Loop. Macro SPACE Loops are performed infrequently – once every six months, once a year, or when you or your organization experiences a significant change. Just as a submarine surfaces in the ocean to check the weather, get its bearings, and take new orders for its mission, Macro SPACE Loops provide the opportunity to step back and reconsider what others *really* want. In a Macro SPACE Loop, you think about the Friction level of your organization and reflect on whether it has changed since your last SPACE Loop. What implications does that have for how you bring forth ideas in meetings or provide differing opinions to your boss? Consider the Sources of Friction in your organization. Have you had a recent situation where you created Heat? Do you recognize the Source of Friction you rubbed against? Are you aware of the Point Sources of Friction which you deal with regularly?

Here are other questions to ask in a Macro SPACE Loop:

- What does your organization *really* want and has this changed recently?
- What do you *really* want and have your *Really* Wants changed recently?
- As the size of your box increases, do you need to reevaluate what you *really* want?
- Are you giving yourself constant reminders to Center Your Ball?
- Are you able to Center Your Ball when needed? Are there creative ways you can keep your *Really* Wants in front of you during your daily routine to improve your ability to keep your ball centered?

Consider executing a Macro SPACE Loop at the beginning of every year as a New Year's resolution. Resolve to give people what they *really* want. Resolve to keep your ball centered. To keep these resolutions, you must understand what your organization *really* wants and what you *really* want. You can then determine what you must do and the ways you must behave to ensure that you avoid creating Heat and thereby increase the size of your box.

SPACE Loops are not simply a once-a-year evaluation. Because SPACE is a continuous process, you must keep SPACE in mind at all times. Use Micro SPACE Loops to ensure that you create SPACE in situations where you are near Friction.

Micro SPACE Loops

Think of a Micro SPACE Loop as one of the computer programs running in your computer's system tray. In the lower-right corner of many computers, you will see icons representing programs that run constantly in the background. These programs perform various functions such as ensuring that you are protected against viruses and monitoring the power usage on a laptop. When they are needed, they are called to the foreground to perform whatever function is requested of them. This is the purpose of a Micro SPACE loop. You run it in the background of your mind and call it into the foreground whenever it is required. Micro SPACE Loops are useful in the presence of Friction to remind you to quickly evaluate what someone *really* wants, remember what you *really* want, Center Your Ball, and act Invisibly. Micro SPACE Loops instruct you to evaluate your options in a situation when you feel Self-Righteous. They ensure that you recognize when you are acting out of Self-Righteousness so you can stop and consider alternatives that will give someone what they *really* want so you can get what you *really* want. This takes place in the midst of situations when you have a choice to convert your Organizational Energy into Heat or into Centering Your Ball.

Example: *AirSPACE*

Micro SPACE Loop

| **Bryant** | **Shelly** |
| Engineer | Engineer |

Bryant works well with most people but becomes annoyed by difficult people. One such person, Shelly, recently moved to Bryant's area. Shelly is disillusioned with AirSPACE and, as a result, supplies negative energy wherever she goes. Because of her attitude, she does not share Bryant's vision to contribute to AirSPACE's success.

Shelly began working closely with others in Bryant's group. In only a few weeks, it was clear that she and Bryant did not have much in common. Her negative energy spread to the rest of the group and he noticed that his colleagues began to complain more often. As time went on, interactions between Bryant and Shelly became tense and strained.

Each AirSPACE employee's schedule is available through the company's computer network so employees can arrange meetings. One afternoon, Bryant was looking through his colleagues' schedules and noticed that Shelly had set up a meeting with three others in Bryant's group to discuss the development of a new production tool ordering system. This tool ordering system would directly impact Bryant's job. Bryant had the most experience with tool ordering throughout the area; his input would be valuable for ensuring that the new system met everyone's needs. However, Shelly deliberately called the meeting without Bryant. She even made a comment in the appointment notice stating that "no others were allowed to attend." It was a clear dig at Bryant, since Bryant had specifically requested to be involved in the system's development.

Bryant was upset and frustrated and his Self-Righteousness ball was elevated. He thought things like: "How dare she set up this meeting without me? She doesn't even belong to our group! She is always negative and doesn't care about doing a good job. For personal reasons, she's shutting me out of something that will directly impact me!" Bryant looked at the clock. The meeting was scheduled to start in five minutes. What should he do?

Certainly, this was an opportunity for Heat Creation. Bryant could show up at the meeting to participate whether they liked it or not. He could come to the meeting just to listen. Here he was, five minutes before the meeting, sitting at his desk with his Self-Righteousness ball elevated. He was ready to create some Heat.

Bryant ran a Micro SPACE Loop. He thought about Probe, Sources of Friction, and what people *really* wanted. He knew that Shelly was a Point Source of Friction. He recognized that she intentionally called this meeting without him. If he attended the meeting, Shelly would use this as a forum to create Heat. Bryant realized that Shelly and he had very different goals. She did not want what he *really* wanted.

Then he thought about what he *really* wanted. He thought about how he would like a promotion. Would attending this meeting help him get a promotion? No, it would not. Even if Shelly developed a poor ordering system, he knew he could work with it. It might not be the most efficient or effective way to operate but he knew that, because of Organizational Mechanics, less of his energy would be transferred to Useful Work. This was just more Friction in the organization and he understood the physics. Then he thought about his other *Really* Wants. He wanted to maximize his time at home with his wife and kids. Would going to this meeting affect his personal time? Well, this new system *could* cause some headaches that would increase the time it takes him to place orders for tools. However, it would not impact his time after work.

On the other hand, if he attended this meeting, he would likely create Heat with his colleagues. He would risk engaging a difficult person. His management would hear of any problems from the meeting and note that people were not getting along. Bryant decided that there were more negative outcomes associated with attending the meeting than there were benefits. He looked at a picture of his family, took a deep breath, centered his ball, and went on with his day.

Everyone knows someone at work who upsets them. Everyone knows someone who they believe is not focused on the organization's best interests. They are frustrating and spread negative energy wherever they go. When working in their presence, keep your ball centered and have Micro SPACE Loops running in your systems tray. A Micro SPACE loop can help you remember that creating Heat simply keeps you from getting what you *really* want.

More on Micro SPACE Loops

Situations that cause your Self-Righteousness ball to move off-center should trigger a Micro SPACE Loop. Anytime you feel Self-Righteous, as in the above example with Bryant and Shelly, bring SPACE to the foreground to determine the best course of action for giving everyone what they *really* want. Another ideal time to run a Micro SPACE Loop is when you have already created Heat. Sometimes it is possible to contain the Heat you have created before it has the chance to shrink your box. It is ideal to avoid creating Heat altogether, but when you do create Heat, run a Micro SPACE Loop to determine your options, as in the example below.

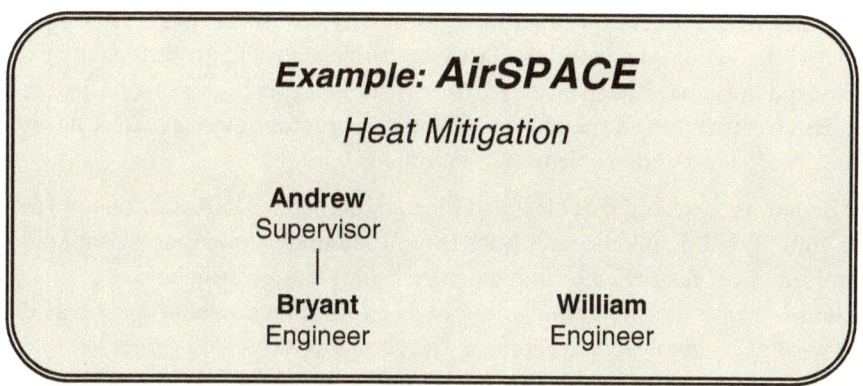

Bryant was leading an effort to implement "visual factory" on one of AirSPACE's engine production lines. Visual factory implementation meant that the factory area must be labeled so, at a glance, anyone can determine what belongs on a shelf or on the floor. For example, to identify the location of a trash can, a circle is drawn around the trash can and the words "trash can" are painted on the floor. Visual factory is an organized way to operate a manufacturing facility.

Bryant's assignment was to implement visual factory on a single production line. Constantly thinking of the future, Bryant expanded the plan to implement the visual factory system throughout the entire department. Bryant knew this would need to be done in the future, anyway. He thought: "Why not do a little extra work now, since we're ordering new shelves and painting floors, rather than spend more energy to restart the effort later?"

When Bryant formed a team, they quickly developed an implementation plan. However, when the team began discussing how to implement visual factory on adjacent lines, William resisted the effort. William, another engineer in the area, disagreed with how a line was configured and wanted it changed before expanding the implementation plan. Bryant did not want to spend the time discussing the configuration change, so he tried to convince William to proceed with the visual factory implementation.

William left one of the meetings upset about the project. Bryant returned to his desk and, shortly thereafter, received a visit from Andrew. Andrew asked what was happening with William and the visual factory project. Bryant immediately understood what had happened. William complained to his own supervisor about the implementation. William's supervisor went to Andrew to pass along William's complaints. Andrew was completing the circuit of communication at Bryant's desk. In AirSPACE's High-Friction environment, this meant that Heat was created. Because of this project, two supervisors were now involved and a colleague on the team was upset. People were not getting what they *really* wanted. For two supervisors, Invisibility Law #2 was being violated (know that the world likes to keep turning). While Bryant may not yet be looked upon negatively by his management, he is the leader of a project that is causing difficulty and frustration. If William becomes more agitated, he will create more Heat and problems for Bryant.

Bryant, recognizing that Heat was created, ran a Micro SPACE Loop. He thought: "What do people *really* want here?" He understood that William did not want visual factory to be implemented on his line because he was dissatisfied with the line's configuration. He knew that the two supervisors did not want to be involved in a problem that should be handled by their employees. He recognized the original assignment was simply to implement visual factory on a single production line. Bryant realized he was creating Heat for something which had nothing to do with his original assignment. He was creating Heat for something nobody *really* wanted! What were his options?

Bryant could continue to push for full visual factory implementation, since this was the most efficient use of AirSPACE's resources in the long term. However, that had already created Heat and would create more before the project was finished. Bryant could also simply stop the project with successful implementation on one engine assembly line, as he was originally asked to do, leaving the rest of the implementation for someone to do in the future. He had already gained concurrence from team members for that option.

Bryant was not entirely satisfied with the second option. He thought: "this is not the *right* way to do this." He realized that his use of the word "right" meant he was feeling Self-Righteous. He remembered the Law of Conservation of Organizational Energy. Work will be accomplished less efficiently than in a Lower-Friction Organization. He realized he could end the project immediately, show himself and the team to be successful, and nobody would question why he did not go further. William would be happy, the team would be successful, and Bryant would get a bigger box. Bryant knew that visual factory would ultimately be implemented on William's line. Bryant may or may not be involved, but good things will still happen; they will just not happen at the speed Bryant had hoped.

Bryant scheduled the next meeting and called it the "successful project closure meeting." He praised the team for their efforts and communicated the project's success to his management. Bryant took a situation where Heat was created and developed an organizationally-friendly solution that gave everyone what they *really* wanted. Bryant felt the Low Level of Pain, since he had to accept the inefficiency of working in a High-Friction Organization. By using Heat-mitigation techniques, he not only avoided shrinking his box, he increased the size of his box with everyone involved.

SPACE Partners

SPACE is something you can learn and practice by yourself. It is effective in High-Friction Organizations because it does not depend on how others behave. When you follow the Laws of Invisibility to avoid creating Heat, you will get a larger box and all the benefits that come with it. However, you can greatly enhance your ability to create SPACE by finding a SPACE partner.

A SPACE Partner is someone who knows you well and whom you trust. When you create SPACE, you must maintain a cool head when someone pushes your buttons. A SPACE Partner knows your hot buttons and can recognize when they have been pushed. They know you well enough to predict how you will react when faced with certain situations. In addition, they know what is important to you, your *Really* Wants, so they can help keep you focused on those goals. Finally, your SPACE Partner is someone you can trust and rely upon to be there for you in emotionally charged situations. You can trust that they will be available for you at High-Friction times when you need them most.

A SPACE partner helps you identify your Self-Righteousness, reminds you what you *really* want during times when you forget, helps you cope with the Low Level of Pain, and assists you in developing organizationally friendly solutions during and after Heat Creation.

Identify your Self-Righteousness

Sometimes it is difficult to recognize when you are acting out of Self-Righteousness. When you are emotionally engaged, it is difficult to be aware of your own Self-Righteousness and make a clear-headed decision on how you should act. When something elevates your Self-Righteousness, it may be hard for you to accurately assess your own behaviors and evaluate your options because of the energy you are losing trying to Center Your Ball.

Your SPACE partner can provide an objective perspective on a situation when you feel Self-Righteous. They can see your Self-Righteousness when you cannot. They know what matters to you and what you become Self-Righteous about. Since they are detached from the immediate situation, they can listen to you and tell you when your elevated Self-Righteousness is clouding your judgment. They can help you work through different options for handling a situation in a way that does not create Heat. Finally, a SPACE Partner can provide valuable empathy when you believe you are being treated unfairly. If you cannot vent your heightened emotions to someone you can trust, you are more likely to let those emotions drive you to create Heat.

A SPACE Partner reminds you that, in spite of the Low Level of Pain you feel, you are getting what you *really* want. They help you avoid creating Heat and keep you focused on what is *really* important to you. When you suggest a course of action that does not help you achieve your goals, they help you adjust your focus and develop a different solution.

Low Level of Pain Coping Strategies

Because a SPACE Partner knows you so well, they can help you create additional Low Level of Pain Coping Strategies. Since they know your *Really* Wants, their creativity may spur new ideas on how to manage the Low Level of Pain of working in a High-Friction Organization.

Dissipate the Heat

Invariably, you will create Heat. You will not create Heat as frequently as you did before, but you will still occasionally rub against Friction. If you act quickly when this happens, you may have the opportunity to dissipate the Heat before it shrinks your box. The clear head of your SPACE Partner can help you think of creative options for mitigating Heat before it becomes a problem for you. When the situation is over, your SPACE Partner can help you analyze the Friction in the situation. They can provide a different perspective for understanding what others *really* want, then help you develop strategies that will keep you from creating Heat the next time you are in a similar situation.

See how a SPACE Partner can help you navigate through a High-Friction situation to choose the approach that creates the least amount of Heat.

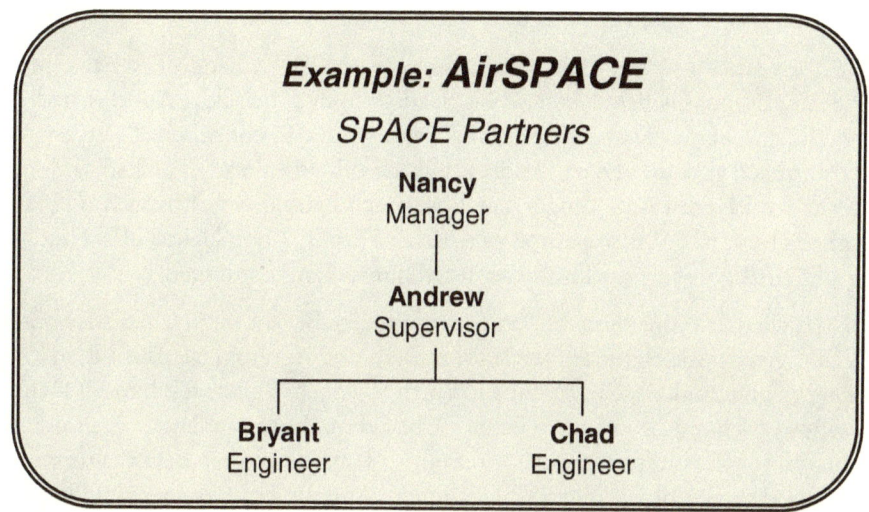

Example: *AirSPACE*

SPACE Partners

Nancy
Manager

Andrew
Supervisor

Bryant
Engineer

Chad
Engineer

AirSPACE is a corporate sponsor of the National Charitable Fund (NCF), a charity that supports development in inner cities. AirSPACE is proud of their involvement with the NCF, advertising their support in annual reports and other corporate press releases. AirSPACE employees are encouraged to make regular donations to the NCF. Donating is, of course, voluntary, but there is pressure within the company to actively contribute. Managers are silently pressured into donating regularly and working-level employees are encouraged in varying degrees.

Bryant has successfully led previous NCF annual campaigns in AirSPACE's Tool Shop. During his first contribution drive, he encouraged the entire Tool Shop to participate, giving them a prestigious 100% participation award. During the current drive, Nancy, the Tool Shop Director, sent an e-mail to the organization asking for everyone's support to reach the 100% participation goal. Everyone in the Tool Shop agreed to participate, except one person.

Andrew saw how effectively Bryant convinced his colleagues to participate. At Nancy's urging, Andrew came to Bryant and asked for his support to achieve the 100% participation goal. Bryant, always eager to do what he could for AirSPACE, agreed. "Who's the holdout?" Bryant asked Andrew. Andrew replied: "Chad."

Bryant took a deep breath. He knew Chad well and knew he was a Point Source of Friction. Chad tried to get an upper hand over Bryant whenever he could. Because Nancy specifically requested Bryant's help, he told Andrew: "I can do that."

Bryant went to Chad's desk. He began: "Hey, Chad, got a minute?"

"What's up?" Chad answered.

Bryant said: "I want to talk to you about the NCF." Chad leaned back into his chair and put his hands behind his head: "Ho ho," he said, "Andrew said you'd be coming to talk to me. Gonna try to get me to contribute?" Bryant was surprised and answered: "Andrew talked with you already?" Chad said: "Yeah. I told him I was going to see how much I could extort from you. He laughed about it." Bryant paused as a Micro SPACE Loop kicked off. He felt a tug of Self-Righteousness but he centered himself and continued.

"So what are your thoughts on contributing?" Bryant said. Chad answered: "Well, I give to the charities *I* want to, not the ones I'm told to. But I'd be willing to give to the NCF. What's it worth to you?" Bryant felt himself losing patience. "What do you want, Chad?" Chad thought for a minute. He said: "I want you to take our group out for pizza." He paused to see Bryant's reaction, who stood there calmly. Then Chad added: "And my little brother is selling these raffle tickets for my Church. I want you to buy two of them." At this point, Bryant lost his patience. He said: "Whatever, Chad," and walked away.

The next day, Bryant received an e-mail from Andrew about the NCF drive. He read from the bottom up. Nancy had sent a note to Andrew asking him the status of the drive. Andrew sent the note to Chad asking whether he would contribute. Chad had replied to Andrew: "Bryant hasn't agreed to my demands for contributing. Eight-ball says: 'Outlook not good.'" Then Andrew forwarded this note to Bryant asking: "Bryant, what are you going to do now???"

Bryant read and reread the message in disbelief. He could not believe Andrew was looking to *him* to solve this problem. Wasn't Chad being difficult here? Didn't everyone know it? Why wasn't anyone coming down on Chad for his behavior? What was going on here?

Bryant was confused and angry and recognized this as a time when he needed some help. He called Jason, his SPACE Partner. Bryant explained the situation, then vented about the absurdity of it. Jason listened patiently. He also knew Chad and agreed that he was a Point Source of Friction. Jason was shocked at Andrew's response to Chad's note. Jason said: "Too bad the hold-out was Chad. Remember Law #6: you do not want to engage a difficult person. So, Bryant, what do you want to do?"

Bryant started thinking out loud: "Well, if I don't do anything, Chad won't contribute. If we don't get the 100% participation, everyone will know that Chad was the one who kept it from happening." Jason listened and said: "Yes, but you see the note they sent you. Nancy *really* wants the 100% participation award. For some reason, they are holding you accountable for Chad's actions. It's funny: even though they know that Chad is playing games, they're making *you* responsible." Bryant grudgingly agreed with Jason's analysis. Observing behaviors revealed critical information buried below the surface. Nobody seemed to be acting reasonably; if they were, Bryant would never have received that e-mail from Andrew. Observing behaviors told him that he, Bryant, would be held accountable if the Tool Shop did not achieve the 100% participation award.

Bryant said: "So what are you saying, Jason? Are you saying I should buy the lunch and the raffle tickets?" Jason answered: "Well, what do you *really* want?" Bryant thought for a minute. He liked having a bigger box. He wanted his management to know that *he* was someone who could make things happen. He wanted the eventual promotion. He thought about his Bottom Lines and none were being violated. Then Jason asked: "How much would all of this cost you if you agreed to it?" Bryant answered: "25 bucks." Jason asked: "How much do you *really* want 25 bucks?" Bryant thought about it. He did not like losing 25 dollars, especially in this way that was so…wrong. When he used the word "wrong," he realized he was feeling Self-Righteous. He answered: "You know, I don't care so much about 25 bucks."

After more discussion with his SPACE partner, Bryant resolved to agree to Chad's demands. He sent an e-mail to Nancy and Andrew saying he was happy to announce that Chad had agreed to support the Tool Shop in their goal to achieve 100% participation. Bryant added that he would schedule the celebration lunch immediately after Chad officially made his donation. He ended the e-mail by congratulating the Tool Shop management on achieving this important goal.

Bryant did not feel good about what he had done until he thought about everything in terms of *Really* Wants. Nancy and Andrew got what they *really* wanted: they achieved their 100% participation goal. Andrew got what he wanted in that he avoided a confrontation with Chad. Bryant recognized that he, himself, got what he *really* wanted: reinforcement to management that if they want something to happen, they can come to him.

Ironically, the only person who did *not* get what he *really* wanted was Chad. He did not *really* want a free lunch and he did not *really* want to sell raffle tickets. He *did* want to put Bryant in an uncomfortable and powerless position. By agreeing to Chad's demands, Bryant took away any power that Chad hoped to gain from the situation. SPACE enabled him to navigate through a difficult situation without creating Heat. Bryant found it poetic that he could satisfy his Self-Righteousness with the knowledge that he did not give a difficult person what they *really* wanted.

Rate of SPACE Creation

Creating SPACE is a continuous process. SPACE is not something you can choose to do one day but not another. Creating Heat once a week is as bad as creating Heat more frequently. This is because the rate of expansion of your box changes depending on the size of your box. When your box is small, it can only expand slowly. As your box gets bigger, it will expand at a faster rate.

If your box is small, it is because you are a Heat Creator. Your management has a very specific opinion of you. Though they may appreciate some of your talents, they also think the following:

- "I do not *fully* trust you to manage something *the way I want it managed.*"
- "Depending on the situation, you are more of a liability than an asset."
- "I expect you to give me a hard time about something instead of doing what I want you to do."
- "I expect you to create Heat."

Success in a High-Friction Organization depends on the expectations others have of how you will behave. If you are a Heat Creator, people simply expect you to create Heat. They have made assumptions based on past experiences of how you will behave. They have developed expectations about how you operate and what you become Self-Righteous about. They expect that, in a situation with Heat Creation potential, you will create Heat. It takes time for you to change their expectations. Whenever you *do* create Heat, it reinforces your management's perception of you as a Heat Creator and keeps your box small.

As you begin to change others' expectations, they will expect you to create less Heat and will give you more freedom and leeway. As you change more of your colleagues' expectations, more will expect you to create SPACE. Your box will expand more quickly.

Example: *AirSPACE*

Rate of SPACE Creation

Kelly
Director

|

Shane
Engineer

Shane, an engineer at AirSPACE, was a Heat Creator who had recently started creating SPACE. He recalled the expression on his director's face when he began using SPACE principles. Shane wanted to interview for a position elsewhere in AirSPACE. He had been offered the interview and was very excited about the opportunity. Unfortunately, it was hard to refill positions when people transferred to other areas and Kelly, his director, thought it was not a good time for him to move. Kelly visited Shane at his cubicle to tell him he could not interview at this time. Shane noticed that Kelly seemed to be waiting for a negative reaction, just as she had received every other time she delivered bad news. Shane just said cheerfully: "I hope that when conditions permit, you'll give me the chance to interview for that job." Shane noticed a bewildered smile on Kelly's face as she walked away. He had just increased the size of his box and started to change Kelly's expectations that he was a Heat Creator.

Increasing the size of your box is a two-step process: you must first *stop* creating Heat, then you must *start* creating SPACE. Once you stop creating Heat, you will slowly begin to change people's perception of you. As you stop creating Heat, you must expect the size of your box to grow slowly. It takes time to alter people's expectations of you as a Heat Creator. However, over time, when you create SPACE instead of Heat, you *will* change those perceptions. The surprised looks from your management will go away as they no longer expect you to create Heat.

As you practice the Laws of Invisibility, especially Law #1 (use conciliation and deference) and Law #4 (give them what they *really* want), you will expand your box even faster. Your management will trust you in more ways. You will get better performance reviews. Your management will give you better assignments. You will find you have the maneuvering room to work for that which is important to you.

> ## Example: *AirSPACE*
> ### *The Effects of a Bigger Box*
>
> **Charlie**
> Engineer

Recall the Probe example where Charlie had a first-hand experience with fear in AirSPACE. Before Charlie was a SPACE Creator, he was placed on an assignment in which he worked with people throughout different areas in AirSPACE. It was an organizational improvement project which had the opportunity to make a significant impact throughout the company. Charlie was uncomfortable with the direction of the project and frequently made his objections known to his management. After only eight weeks in his assignment, he was abruptly removed and placed into a job where he did not interface with anyone outside of his immediate building. He found himself in a very limited area with little opportunity to make an impact.

Then Charlie began to create SPACE. Over time, his box got bigger and Charlie's management began to trust him to do his work in a way that did not create Heat. A year after Charlie's ill-fated assignment, another organizational improvement project was established. Because Charlie was now a SPACE Creator, his management picked him to work on the project. His supervisor went with him to the initial meeting. After one hour, Charlie's supervisor was satisfied that he would manage the project in a way that was organizationally friendly. Charlie's supervisor left the meeting, leaving Charlie as the lone representative from his organization. Charlie had received confirmation that he had expanded his box and gained his management's trust.

If you have truly changed your management's perception of you, your box will expand more quickly. You will have more leeway in daily situations and your management will be more forgiving of a single Heat Creation situation. In a High-Friction Organization, there is so much opportunity to create Heat that, invariably, everyone creates Heat *occasionally*. However, that leeway will not last long if you *continue* to create Heat.

SPACE Maps

SPACE Maps tie together the entire SPACE approach into a single tool. SPACE Maps help you navigate Friction to determine an optimal solution for giving your organization what it *really* wants and for getting what you *really* want. A SPACE Map guides you through each phase of SPACE, documenting the outcomes of each phase in an easy-to-visualize diagram. When the SPACE Map is complete, it will help clarify your thoughts so you can pick the right approach for giving your organization what it *really* wants and getting what you *really* want.

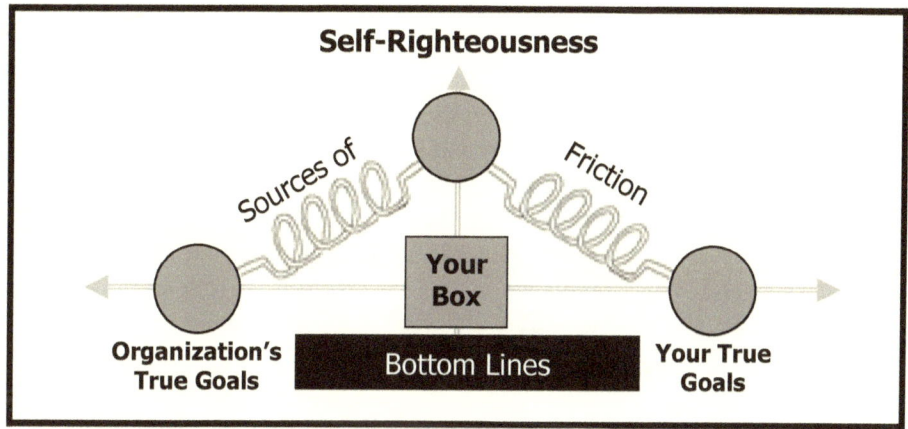

SPACE Map

To create a SPACE Map:

1) Begin by listing what your organization *really* wants and what you *really* want.

2) Look at your list of *Really* Wants. Refine your list until they are all SPACEable.

3) List the Sources of Friction present in the situation.

4) List items in your box that you can control and manage (your maneuvering room).

5) List your feelings that you recognize as Self-Righteousness.

6) Enter your Bottom Lines to remind you of your limits for acting Invisibly.

When you use a SPACE Map in a Friction-filled situation, you have all the information in a single location to enable you to get what you *really* want. You will be able to compare your *Really* Wants with your organization's *Really* Wants; you will often find they are compatible. You will see the landmines in your organization that will cause you pain if you do not avoid them. By documenting your Self-Righteous feelings, you will see very clearly that they are emotional responses which do not help you get what you *really* want.

The conclusion to the AirSPACE Tool Shop Utilization Report Example at the end of this chapter will show how a SPACE Map is used to tie together the SPACE tools and help you find the optimal solution to a situation.

Execute - Conclusions

Execute is a set of tools to help you focus on managing your interface with your organization. Because High-Friction Organizations value behaviors over results, you must continuously focus on *how* you deliver your work to your organization. Execute tools will give you strength to keep your ball centered through difficult situations. Execute tools will ensure that you maximize the amount of Useful Work you do in your organization. Most importantly, when you begin feeling the success and satisfaction from a bigger box, Execute will prevent you from going back to your old interface and behaviors which did not work for you.

If you regularly use Execute tools, you will find it easier to create SPACE naturally. Execute tools help you prioritize what is truly important to you. They remind you that working in a High-Friction Organization is difficult. They also remind you that the physics of your organization is not perfect, so you should expect to do some Non-Useful Work. They reinforce the Laws of Invisibility, which will enable you to work without creating Heat. Execute tools help you work in a way that your entire organization, from your supervisors to your colleagues and your subordinates, will appreciate.

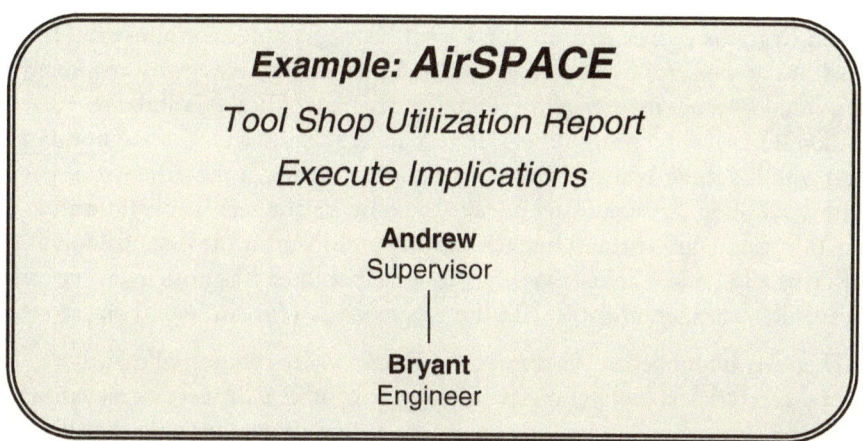

Bryant decided to develop a SPACE Map for the situation with the Tool Shop Utilization report to guide him to the best solution for everyone.

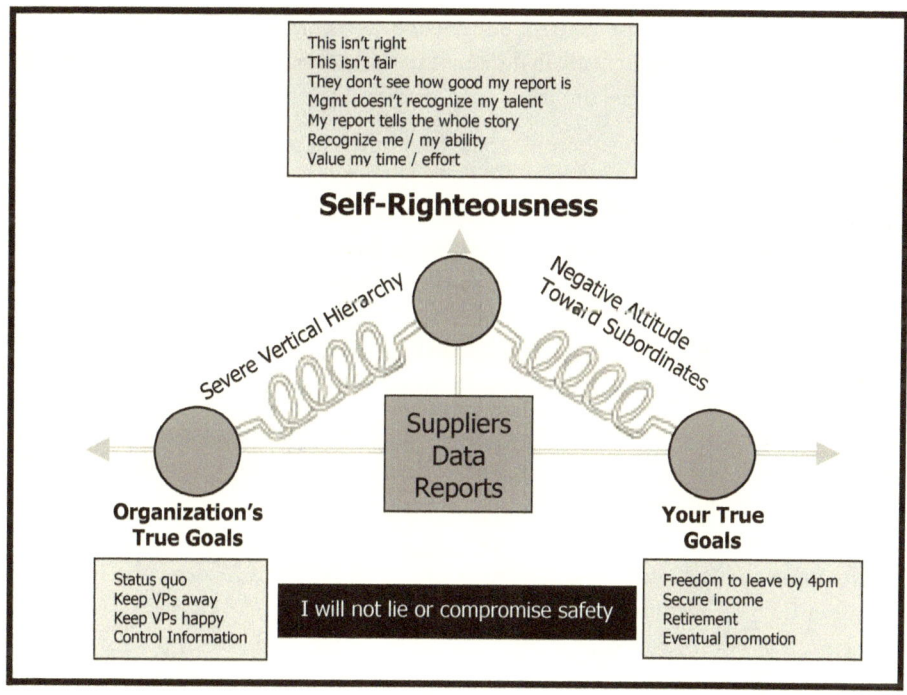

SPACE Map for the Tool Shop Utilization Report Example

Bryant started by listing everyone's true goals. Bryant believed that Andrew's goal was to create an overly positive perception of the Tool Shop. Andrew had stated that he wanted the vice-presidents of AirSPACE to have no reason to return to the facility. Bryant was certain this was what Andrew *really* wanted from the report. Bryant knew what he *really* wanted for himself. He wanted to go home at a reasonable time and maintain his energy for his family. He wanted a secure income and eventual retirement. He also wanted to position himself for a promotion. He recognized that this report had nothing to do with his *Really* Wants. Whether he counted chairs in the cafeteria or parts in the Tool Shop, he would still be able to go home at a reasonable time and have that secure income and retirement. Bryant looked at the organization's true goals and looked at his own. He noticed that there was nothing in his own goals which was incompatible with the organization's (or Andrew's) goals.

Then Bryant looked at the Sources of Friction. He recognized that there was a severe vertical hierarchy; that is, people at AirSPACE were expected to ask for permission from upper management for decisions they were capable of making themselves. He also recognized a negative attitude towards subordinates. These two Sources of Friction reminded him that his management was not looking for dissenting opinions; rather, they just wanted him to do what he was told.

He then listed items he controlled. He worked with suppliers to the Tool Shop. He managed and controlled data. He developed various reports. These items, he recognized, were the tools he controlled for managing his job.

He listed his thoughts when Andrew told him to count blades of grass. He thought: "This isn't right! This isn't fair!" He was frustrated that he was not being recognized for his skills and talents in creating such an effective report. When he looked at everything he had written, he realized he was especially frustrated by the lack of recognition for doing what he knew was a great job. He thought about this and remembered that "doing a great job" is not a SPACEable *Really* Want. Being recognized for doing a great job was not something he could expect in AirSPACE without being frustrated.

Finally, Bryant wrote that he would not lie or compromise safety. Clearly, counting blades of grass in front of the office would not compromise safety. However, would he be lying if he did not present the data he developed in the original report? He would not put data on blades of grass on the report. Was there some data he *could* present that was truthful *and* gave Andrew the big number he *really* wanted? There were many different types of data he could present; that choice was certainly within his box. He could easily give Andrew what he *really* wanted if he just centered his ball and thought creatively of other options.

In the end, Bryant developed a report which had big, good-looking numbers, just as Andrew had requested. The report did not contain the numbers Bryant believed were the right ones to manage the Tool Shop, but the report did not contain data on blades of grass, either. The numbers on the report were not directly relevant but they were not useless. Perhaps some good would eventually come from the report; it just would not happen as fast as Bryant wanted.

This situation, combined with countless other daily situations, helped Bryant increase the size of his box. Over time, he created the freedom and maneuvering room to work in a way that helped him attain that which was most important to him.

Key Points from Execute:

1) Always be aware of your Invisibility to ensure that you work without creating Heat.

2) The Credit Trap can cause you to revert to your old behaviors which were not valued by your organization.

3) Macro SPACE loops help you regularly ensure that your *Really* Wants stay fresh and relevant.

4) Micro Space Loops run constantly, ready to stop you from creating Heat.

5) A SPACE Partner is a valuable teammate in your efforts to increase the size of your box and get what you *really* want.

6) You must practice SPACE continuously because, when you create Heat, it is more difficult to start expanding your box again.

7) SPACE Maps lay out a difficult situation to show you the optimal solution for giving others what they *really* want and getting what you *really* want.

Execute completes the SPACE Strategy. You have everything you need to change how you feel about going to work every day. You have what you need to start maximizing your impact at work and end your frustration. You are ready to tune your interface so you work in a way that your organization will really appreciate. You will give your organization what it *really* wants. More importantly, you will get what you *really* want.

CONCLUSION

Life is too short to not get what you *really* want.

SPACE gives you a set of tools for success, regardless of the organization you are in. Any group you work with will appreciate the interface that SPACE will help you create.

By Creating SPACE, you will maximize the impact of your Organizational Energy. You will help those around you maximize the impact of their Organizational Energy. Your coworkers will appreciate you more. Your organization will appreciate you more. You will be more satisfied at work.

Start enjoying the freedom of a bigger box. Start enjoying the satisfaction of knowing that your valuable energy is going towards what is truly important to you.

Create SPACE. Get what you *really* want at work.

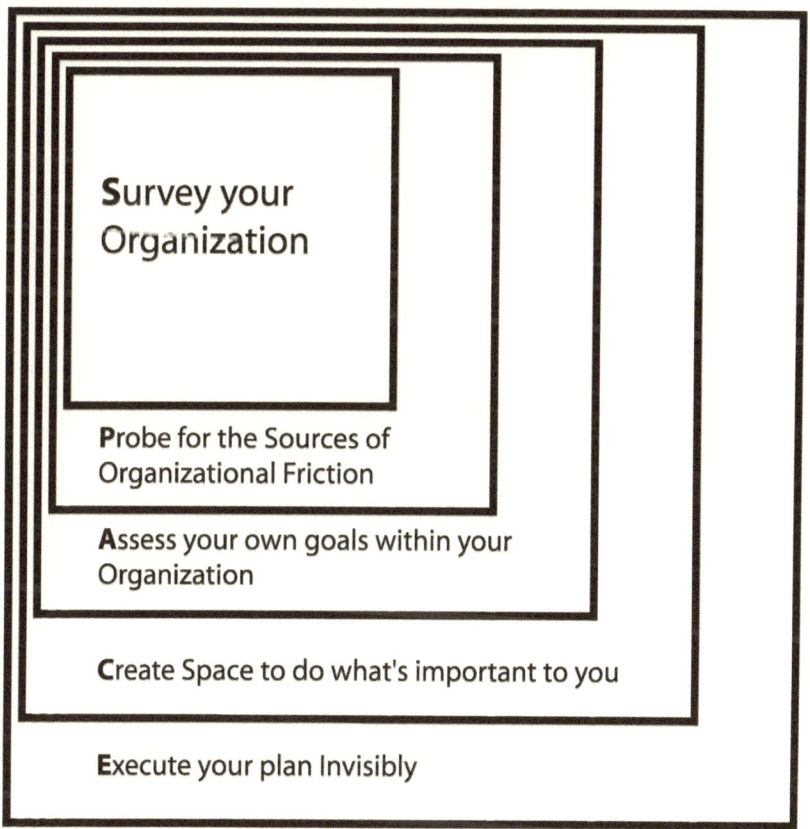

To order additional copies, visit http://frozenyams.com/CreateSPACE.

Frozen Yams offers seminars and career coaching. Visit www.frozenyams.com
for more information.

For corrections or comments, send e-mails to createspace@frozenyams.com.

We'd love to hear your SPACE success stories. Send them to
success@frozenyams.com.

www.ingramcontent.com/pod-product-compliance
Lightning Source LLC
Chambersburg PA
CBHW022231290526
45785CB00014B/716